F*CK CANCER

COMMANDING A COMEBACK WHEN YOUR BODY HAS TURNED ON YOU

By

FARLA EFROS
THE HEALING REBEL CA

F*ck Cancer: Commanding a Comeback When Your Body Has Turned On You

Written by Farla Efros

Design and cover art by Peaceful Profits.

Paperback ISBN: 978-1-967587-87-2
eBook ISBN: 978-1-967587-88-9
Hardcover ISBN: 978-1-967587-89-6

This book is a work of nonfiction. It represents the accuracy of the events mentioned to the best of the author's recollection. Some names in the book have been replaced to maintain the privacy of certain individuals.

The business information contained in this book is provided for educational purposes only and should not be construed as legal, financial, tax, or investment advice. Readers are strongly encouraged to consult with a qualified and licensed professional who can provide advice tailored to their individual circumstances. Laws, regulations, and financial practices vary across countries, states, and regions. Market conditions, returns, and outcomes will differ over time and cannot be guaranteed. While every effort has been made to provide accurate and timely information at the time of writing, we make no representations or warranties regarding completeness, accuracy, or applicability. We are not making any official legal or financial recommendations.

The medical information contained in this book is provided for educational purposes only and should not be construed as medical advice. Readers are strongly encouraged to consult with a qualified and licensed professional who can provide advice tailored to their individual circumstances. Laws, regulations, and medical practices vary across countries, states, and regions. While every effort has been made to provide accurate and timely information at the time of writing, we make no representations or warranties regarding completeness, accuracy, or applicability. We are not making any official medical recommendations. The examples, figures, and principles presented herein are for illustrative and educational purposes only. Any decisions you make are solely your responsibility.

DEDICATION

For **Mik**, my husband—thank you for standing in the fire with me, for loving me through the fear, the fatigue, and the fierceness. You never asked me to be strong; you simply believed I already was.

For **Arielle**, my daughter—my why, my light, my reminder that love outshines even the darkest days. Watching you chase your dreams has been my greatest healing.

For my **sister**, gone too soon, whose courage lives in every brave thing I do.

For my **father**, who drifted away in slow motion—Alzheimer's took the map but not the love.

For my **mother**, who fought brain cancer with a lion's heart and still worried about me until her last breath.

And for the **warriors**—every scarred, beautiful soul fighting their way forward.

You are not alone in this fire.

And to the ones who thought they could break me—

I'm still here. Still standing. Fuck you.

This is for the rebels who choose to heal out loud.

TABLE OF CONTENTS

I never thought I'd have to fight for my life while losing everything that once grounded me. Cancer didn't just come for my body—it came for my peace, my security, my family. In one year, I lost my hair, my breasts, my ovaries, my fallopian tubes, my parents, my sense of safety, and some days, my will to keep going. But I never lost myself. Not fully. And that's where this story begins—in the rubble, with a whisper of rebellion and a refusal to disappear.

–Farla Efros

CANCER DIDN'T KNOCK

Cancer didn't knock.

It slid in—

quiet, sudden,

like a door I didn't see until I was standing in it.

One moment,

I was living the life I'd always known.

The next?

Everything changed.

That door didn't just open.

It **shifted** me.

Shook me.

Split the timeline.

Before cancer,

I was always moving.

Working.

Pushing.

Checking boxes.

There was always something next.

Always later.

But later never came.

Because cancer came first.

And in its stillness,

I finally stopped.

Not by choice.

But by necessity.

And when I stopped—

I could finally hear.

Feel.

See.

The noise faded.

The distractions dropped.

And the question rose:

"What really matters?"

Not the deadlines.

Not the titles.

Not the to-do list that never ends.

What matters…

is family.

The ones who show up when everything else falls apart.

The ones who don't need you to be strong—

just *real*.

What matters…

is friends.

The ones who hold your hand through the hard.

Who sit with your silence.

Who make you laugh when your body aches from crying.

What matters…

is laughter—

not in spite of pain,

but as a way through it.

Laughter that reminds you—

you're still here.

Still human.

Still *you*.

And what matters most

is this:

Experience.

This moment.

This breath.

This sky.

This hand in yours.

This coffee.

This soft wind.

This tiny miracle of now.

I spent so many years rushing past it all.

Too busy to notice the roses,

let alone stop to smell them.
But cancer?
It made me stop.
It didn't just threaten my life—
It handed it back to me,
with a different kind of clarity.
And now, I walk forward,
through this sliding door,
into a life I never planned…
but finally understand.
Because now,
I choose.

PROLOGUE

I didn't start writing as The Healing Rebel CA on social media because I had free time or needed a hobby. I wasn't looking to build an audience or slap some hashtags on my pain.

I started writing because I was tired of just surviving. Beating aggressive Stage 2 breast cancer was the goal, and I won the prize, but now what?

I used to be a president, commanding boardrooms and strategizing with major companies. Now I'm lucky if my hips listen when I command them to stand my body upright.

Before cancer, I dressed in my carefully curated designer clothes, packed my luxury luggage, and set off down the jetway to the next company in crisis. I'm still wearing designer clothes, but now it's more like comfort couture.

Cancer closed the door on the life I had, the woman I was, and pushed me into an alternate reality. Don't get me wrong, I'm still me. But cancer was my sliding door, and I have different priorities now.

Somewhere between a double mastectomy, a menopause-inducing hormone blocker called letrozole, and what I now call my "post-apocalyptic Barbie" phase, I realized: I'm not merely surviving. I'm inspiring. I never imagined that writing as The Healing Rebel CA on social media would touch so many people. I just needed an outlet. But the titanic-sized boatload of positive feedback I've received from my sometimes snarky, but always genuine, narrative was encouraging. So I kept going.

This isn't a story of endurance. This is the story of how one woman's fight became a movement. It's a sign to others who are struggling in the aftermath of winning the fight but still fighting daily battles.

Every day, I wake up in a body that feels like it was designed by an evil committee of scientists who hated joints, forgot how elbows should work, and said, "What if we just lit up her fingers like fireworks every morning?"

And still, I get up.

Some days I stretch. Some days I swear. Some days I slap on an '80s playlist, channel my inner Cyndi Lauper, and remind myself: Girls just wanna have functional hips.

I drink the tart cherry juice. I pop the Claritin. I down magnesium like it's candy from an aerobics instructor wearing leg warmers.

I go to osteopaths, massage therapists, and acupuncturists, and I once seriously considered cupping therapy for my face when someone told me it would relieve the pain.

Hell, if someone told me strapping on a parachute and jumping out of a plane would make the bone pain disappear, I'd do it. I'm terrified of heights, but I'd scream "Livin' On a Prayer" all the way down if it meant landing with knees that didn't ache.

Because the truth is: This isn't just about me.

It's about all of us who have to rebuild our lives in a post-cancer body, figuring out what works, what hurts, and what helps.

To those of you who don't have pain on these meds: I'm in awe of you. You're the unicorns of Aromatase Inhibitor Land. I hope you're dancing your pain-free butts off to Wham! in your living room. But I also know you've probably battled in other ways. There's no one-size-fits-all version of this journey.

To those of us in pain, still on the meds, trying desperately not to lose ourselves in the process—I see you.

This is my story, and I hope you'll find inspiration, motivation, and the strength to keep going.

PART 1

It's Cancer

INTRODUCTION

I t's cancer.

The call to my husband was short. Not because we didn't have a million things to say, but because he was in the hotel room with me when I got the news.

We were in Valencia, Spain, meeting his dad for a vacation from Spain to Morocco. I had been on a conference call with a major athleisure brand, doing what I do best—preparing to save another company in crisis.

But my second phone rang, and I recognized the number on the screen. It was my high-risk doctor. I had a feeling that I was about to be the one in crisis.

I've been part of a high-risk program since I was 41 years old—about 12 years—due to a history of cancer in my family. I come from a very bad gene pool, even though I am a negative gene carrier, meaning I don't carry an inherited mutation known to increase cancer risk. I took the Tyrer-Cuzick Risk Assessment (available at https://MagView.com). It uses your personal family history to estimate your risk of developing breast cancer, and I had genetic testing done.

Being in the high-risk program meant I would go in for a mammogram and an MRI every six months to a year. Not because the little robes were so couture, but because I wasn't taking chances.

During this time, I was occasionally called back into the doctor's office over a suspicious-looking something, and they would take a biopsy. The results always came back normal.

Just before we left for the trip, I had undergone a routine mammogram followed by an MRI. The mammogram showed clear results, but the MRI revealed two spots. They called me in for a biopsy on one of the spots before my trip. I was to do the next one upon my return.

But now, it seemed the results of that biopsy had come in—right in the middle of a conference call with this major brand.

I politely excused myself from the call, grabbed my other phone, and slid my thumb across the screen.

"Hello?"

"Farla. It's Dr. Lennox."

Her words reverberated through the line as she got straight to the point.

"This is a very painful and hard call I have to make, but your biopsy came back. You have cancer."

"But my mammogram was clear. My mammogram was clear." I kept repeating the phrase as if it were a lifeline that would save me from the free fall—stop the world from spinning.

"Are you alone?" she asked. (She should have led with that!)

"No. My husband is here."

Mik and I have been through a lot in the past couple of years. His real name is Mike, but I've always known him as Mik. While playing hockey, he went into cardiac arrest. I was notified on WhatsApp while flying at 30,000 feet. We had also lost my sister to cancer—so much pain—but this was different.

When I hung up, I think I just said, "It's cancer."

Then silence.

And then, in his steady voice, "Okay. We fight."

I got dressed, and we went out to dinner. What else was there to do?

Denial wears a pantsuit, my friends. And she's punctual.

It took a while for reality to hit. In a state of shock, I logged into the MyChart patient portal to view my biopsy results. It was supposed to be routine. My mammogram was clear after all.

But there it was in black and white: invasive ductal cancer, intermediate grade, awaiting further pathology. It would be a couple more weeks before the final pathology was completed. The death knell that made it all too real.

And then…there were phone calls to make. People to notify. My daughter, my parents, and my brother.

Telling my daughter was the hardest thing I've ever done.

This is the girl I raised between red-eye flights and late-night recitals. The one I once met halfway at an airport just to hug her between client meetings. The one I sat beside, pretending I wasn't working while secretly answering emails on my phone under the table.

She's the love of my life, and the idea that I could be taken from her? Unthinkable.

So I called her. FaceTime. She was attending medical school in Ireland. Ironically, we had just taken her and her friends out to dinner the day before.

"I have breast cancer," I said. "But here's the deal. I've been fighting boardrooms full of men twice my size and half my skill for 30 years. I've flown through turbulence scarier than this. And I'm not going anywhere without a fight."

She looked at me and said, "Okay, then we fight. We got this."

Sidenote: I knew she was mine.

The Diagnosis Dress Code

You know what no one tells you about cancer?

That one day you're buying a power suit, and the next, you're Googling, "Does chemo go with heels?"

(Answer: No one really knows—but I made it work.)

The day I was diagnosed, I didn't cry. I didn't scream. I didn't crumble. Not that day.

I did what any highly trained, achievement-oriented, fix-it-all executive woman does: I ordered a large three-ring binder on Amazon. Heavy-duty. With pockets. And then I asked for a second opinion. Then a third.

My mind went straight to logistics—a fancy word for the mundane tasks of planning, coordinating, and implementing all the details of an operation. But it's not mundane to me. *This is where I thrive.*

What hospital? Which surgeon? What oncologist? What's the timeline?

How can I still make the Q3 meeting?

It was like I thought I could schedule cancer—as if it was just another board meeting that needed prep and a strong closing slide.

I walked into those first appointments dressed like I was headed to court to defend myself—blazer, blowout, and an emotional support handbag that cost more than my first car. Because if I was going down, I was going down in style.

But cancer has a way of stripping all of that.

The labels. The armor. It's all an illusion of control.

One day, you're commanding a boardroom, and the next, you're standing half-naked in a freezing exam room while someone you've never met measures your breasts with a ruler and talks about margins and lymph nodes like it's a typical Tuesday.

Let me tell you something about being a high-functioning woman who's always had the answers: There is nothing more destabilizing than realizing you cannot out-plan, outthink, or outwork your own body.

People think cancer is the hardest part. It's not.

It's the silence that follows your diagnosis. The people who say, "I'm here for you," but disappear the moment it gets uncomfortable. It's the messages that stop, the invitations that never come once promised, the way people justify their distance with phrases like, "I didn't know what to say," or "You seemed so strong," or "I'm sorry." I'm sorry for what? That it didn't happen to you?

Let me be clear—strength doesn't mean I didn't need you.

Some of the deepest wounds I carry were never made by a scalpel or chemo. They were made by people I trusted—people I believed would stand by me, people who saw my vulnerability, but stepped back instead of forward.

Well, reader, this is me stepping forward for you.

This isn't just another cancer book. Sure, I'm going to tell my story because it needs to be told. Maybe you're here because you need to hear it.

But you have your own story. You might be flying through the storm clouds right now wondering if you'll survive. *Is there really a silver lining?*

Cancer will make you work for everything. And I mean everything. But if you're willing to fight, I'm going to help you get through it.

Your Preflight Instructions

I'm like the flight attendant giving preflight instructions. Only this time, you'll want to pay attention.

If you do, you'll learn how to be a confident advocate for yourself or your loved one at every single appointment, which is jotted down in your Moleskine planner. I'll show you how to make an agenda for every meeting, so all of your questions get answered, and important information is documented.

You'll learn how to adopt a leadership mindset to make informed decisions even when they seem impossible.

I'll show you how to negotiate for any test you want, even if it's "not typically done."

You'll be able to put a plan into action like you're Sara Blakely launching Spanx to a room full of men—because you will have to be.

And you'll learn what it means to gather a support system—one that actually steps up when you need it instead of hiding out in the supply closet, scrolling through memes.

By the end of this book, you'll have cried the ugly tears, screamed a few profanities, and wept as curses reverberated off the shower walls; but most of all, you'll see the sun break through the darkest clouds.

If you're a friend, family member, or spouse supporting a loved one through this labyrinth of emotions, meetings, and "what the f*ck" moments, this book will give you the tools you need to be the calm, confident voice of reason amid the chaos. I want you to know that you're not alone and you can do this. It all comes down to the fight.

For me, it was one phrase, one mantra that I hugged to my chest every minute of every day: I Don't Want to Die.

It was my guiding light, my true north.

I've walked the cancer path before with my mother and my sister—in my heels and Chanel. Now, I've got a brand new pair of Louboutins fresh out of the box.

Let's take the next step together.

CHAPTER 1

Denial Is in the House

I'm standing in my closet, staring at a row of dresses I might never wear again. Ones that show off a body I know I'm about to lose. I pull one off the rack, my favorite, and hold it up against me. I love the way this one drapes, as if it were cut just for me.

I gather my long blonde hair in my other hand and twist it into an updo. As I stare at my reflection in the mirror, my eyes follow the neckline as it plunges into a V.

Stage 2B, Triple Positive Aggressive. Fast moving.

This dress wasn't made for a flat-chested woman. It was made to show off curves. My curves. And now, what will happen to my curves—my breasts?

Grade 2, Estrogen Positive 100%, Progesterone Positive 60%, and HER2-Positive [triple positive]

Somehow, my brain recalls the exact pathology. A string of letters and numbers; a code for cancer. Meaningless to the unknowing. I silently wish I were still among the unknowing.

For years, I was the woman in heels and a blazer, dragging a carry-on and a laptop full of crisis plans.

I need a crisis plan.

Back then, I was unstoppable. I was interim CEO by breakfast, Chief Restructuring Officer by lunch, and still back in time (barely) for a bedtime story—at least over FaceTime. Dinner came with a side of business. I was president of a consulting firm, always performing multiple roles at the same time. I've restructured more companies than I can count, advised boardrooms, driven growth strategies, and walked into absolute corporate chaos…smiling. It was high-functioning madness—and I thrived in it!

After all that? My business partner and I sold our company.

Not just sold it—sold it right. The kind of sale that doesn't just set you up, it sets your people up too. Every employee had a place. Contractually, I had to stay for three years, and then I had the option to extend if I wanted. Top of Chanel. Top of Louis Vuitton. For once, I thought I might actually take a breath. I made it two years before the storm.

And then, like a punch to the chest—breast cancer.

No warning. No time to ease into it. Just: *You have cancer.* And everything tilted sideways.

You think that when you've worked this hard, built this much, sacrificed like hell, that life should cut you a break. You think you've paid your dues. That surely the universe would give you a little grace after all the red-eye flights, boardroom fires, and hotel-lobby therapy sessions.

But cancer doesn't care.

It doesn't care how prepared you are or how many spreadsheets you've built.

I need a spreadsheet!

No matter how organized your calendar is, cancer shows up uninvited, and it doesn't knock.

So here I stand. In a closet full of gorgeous dresses. Staring back at a woman who is about to be forever changed, as I lose my grasp on what I thought my future would hold. My dress slips from my hands and puddles at my feet, and I crumple to the floor with the weight of it all.

That's the thing no one warns you about. The grief before the grief.

Before the hair falls out. Before the scars are carved. Before the hormone therapy that screws with your mind and your soul and your everything. Before the aches and pains that keep reminding you that you are held hostage by this disease. And the unbidden thought, *Will I ever be free?*

There's a slow unraveling that happens in silence. Behind closed doors. Alone. Between text messages and appointment reminders.

But even in that unraveling, I wasn't broken.

I was pissed. I was hurt.

I was scared.

But I was still me.

I knew—somewhere deep beneath the anger, the confusion, the spreadsheet of side effects—that this was going to change everything. Whether I wanted it or not.

But I also knew: Cancer had no idea who it was dealing with.

Just Call Me the Chaos Coordinator

Cancer is chaos. There's really no other way to put it. It brandishes a sledgehammer and plays whack-a-mole with everything in your life.

But I know how to deal with chaos. I have been training for this for 30 years. My background as a retail turnaround specialist prepared me for how I would approach this new midlife dumpster fire.

So please, cancer, take a seat. I'm here, and I'm running the show now.

Within hours of hearing the diagnosis in that hotel in Valencia, I had called friends and family. I had reviewed my labs. I had ordered a binder and started planning how to navigate through my new project: Me.

I remember sitting in the consultation room, nodding politely while my oncologist walked me through my treatment plan. Chemo. Multiple Surgeries. Hormone therapy. Bone cancer prevention therapy. Possibly radiation. It would be a long road and an aggressive approach.

She was calm, empathetic, and methodical.

I was…already mentally color-coding my calendar.

Like, okay, so we start chemo here—six rounds—spacing them every three weeks. Looking ahead, that means—yes!—I could still fit in that retreat I had planned. Maybe I'll just move the panel to a Zoom meeting. No big deal.

Did I introduce you to Denial? Oh, yeah, that's my alter-ego. She rides a flying unicorn and sprinkles rainbow dust over my head anytime the hard truth comes knocking.

So yeah. Denial was in the house, but so was Farla, the Chaos Coordinator. And thankfully, cooler heads prevailed.

On the Corner of Hope and Despair

When you come to a crossroads like this, you can take the path of "woe is me," or you can strut down the street called "I'm going to get ahead of this." And that's exactly what I did. I decided to treat my cancer diagnosis and treatment plan like the most important consulting project I've ever had. Because it was.

Instead of listening to a talking head tell me what was best for me, I brought the main character energy. Not just the main character, but the director too.

I went into every meeting with every doctor holding an agenda. Two copies: one for me and one for the doctor. Then I went from meeting to meeting with a recap of prior meetings and notes on everything I had done in between meetings. Lots of meetings. Lots of notes.

Every appointment with every specialist became a strategic two-way conversation—an open dialogue. I initiated conversations by saying, "These are the things I want to do, and here's how I want to approach it."

No unhinged, wild-eyed, sleep-deprived patient in sight. Just a cool, calm, and collected chaos coordinator doing what she does best: putting out little fires everywhere while wearing a designer jumpsuit.

Chaos Controlled: Ready on the Flight Deck

That's what I want you to take away from this book. Just because your world is crashing down around you doesn't mean you have to go with it.

I'm going to show you how to become a confident advocate for yourself, no matter how many specialists are staring down at you and shaking their heads. You might have someone who can support you at every appointment, but you might not. Learning to speak up and ask questions, even when you're not sure what you're talking about, is crucial to getting the help you need.

I'll teach you how to strategize with your doctors to create an optimized plan of action while gaining their respect as an informed patient. Because being informed of your options is critical. Every option has its pros and cons. What works for another might not work for you. It's up to you to follow your gut instincts and come armed with research.

You'll see that even highly motivated, I-can-do-it-all-myself overachievers need a support team. From chemo dance parties and belting out '80s Top 40 tunes to quiet lunches in side-street cafés, having good people around you helps keep you out of your head.

So if you're feeling a little unbalanced, like the air is being sucked from the room, take a minute to scream into your pillow if you want to. I'll deploy the oxygen masks.

Good. Now wipe that mascara off your cheek, fix your lipstick, and straighten your hair. We've got work to do.

No matter where you are right now—stuck, paralyzed with fear—you don't have to stay that way. I've got you! We're kicking Denial out the door without a parachute. She's not coming back.

It's time to raid the supply closet—we're professionals, and we don't go to meetings unprepared. You'll need to arm yourself with a good planner, a three-ring binder, notebooks, pens, highlighters, and sticky notes.

Get the fancy ones; you deserve it.

Welcome to the Club No One Wants to Join (AKA The C Club)

I see you. Standing at the door, peeking around the corner. You're not sure if you're in the right place, even though the sign on the door says, "The C Club."

Yes, if you recently got a cancer diagnosis, as I did, or if someone you care about just shared the devastating news, you're in the right place. Or maybe you're dealing with another type of life-changing illness; we welcome all brands.

Today is initiation day, and you feel as if you've just been dropped into a parallel universe. It's an out-of-body experience that I like to call a sliding door.

One minute you're booking meetings with name-brand companies while arriving just in the nick of time for your daughter's recital, and the next minute you're a full-fledged, card-carrying member of The C Club.

C for Cancer, yes. But also C for Chaos. C for Crying in the shower. C for Control—completely gone. C for "Can't believe this is my life right now."

You're in the club now, although you really don't want to be. None of us do. No one signs up for this. No one applies to be a member of the club, much less to be the club president. (Not saying I'm the president, but I probably could be!)

A cancer diagnosis is a lot to take in: the fear, the fog, the endless internet rabbit holes. Once you're inducted into the club, you can't unsubscribe. Like "Hotel California," your name is on the guest list in permanent ink. But you can learn to navigate it, and that's where this book comes in. Perhaps someone gave you this copy. Maybe you were doomscrolling Facebook at 3:00 a.m., and it popped up. Either way, it's your new lifeline.

The C Club doesn't come with a manual. If it did, it wouldn't be glossy and color-coded. It would be dog-eared, wine-stained, and half-written in sarcasm with a Sharpie.

This book is my version of that. It will give you clarity, confidence, and community because there's more to The C Club than cancer and chaos. I'm not a doctor. I'm not a therapist. I'm just a woman who got that phone call at the height of her career.

Once the shock wears off—just a little—you're going to want a plan. That's when you add that binder to your Amazon shopping list. Because, as much as this sucks, you've got choices to make. The first one is: *How do I move forward from here?*

I spent decades solving crises for businesses as a president and CEO. But this isn't just another day at the office. So, what did I do? I got down to business.

Patient Care 101: It's Not About the Stage

You've got hurdles ahead. Not the kind you trained for, and not the kind you can clear with an iced cappuccino in one hand and a Birkin bag in the other. But you will need to be organized, thoughtful, and pragmatic if you want to win this race.

Before cancer called, my job was to fix things that were falling apart. But nothing prepares you for your own body betraying you. It's not that I didn't try. I did everything right. I took care of my body like it was a one-of-a-kind Hermès Kelly bag. I exercised, ate nutritious foods, and rested with both eyes closed and my phone in Do Not Disturb mode. But still, cancer came for me.

At that moment, I knew one thing: I didn't want to die. My type of cancer has a good survival rate, but not everyone gets that option. Some are handed a terminal prognosis.

The thing is, you get to choose how you fight—how you'll make the best of what you've been given. And that's power.

I chose to fight with a highlighter as my sword and a three-ring binder as my shield. I assembled my little army of people like I was marching into battle. Because I was. I went into every meeting prepared. And so must you.

Focus on the Plan, Not the Stage

Your story might begin with a phone call, like mine, or you might receive the news while sitting in the doctor's office, hands shaking, head spinning. After the initial shock, the first question asked is usually, "What stage?"

Everyone hears "Stage 4," and their mind jumps to the worst. But let's be real. Stage 4 isn't always a death sentence, and Stage 1 isn't always a walk in the park. Cancer doesn't follow a flight plan.

Instead of obsessing over the stage, focus on the plan. What's the next step? Is there a strategy for treatment? How do you move forward from here?

Because survival is the goal, and it's more than just a number on a scan. To survive this thing, you need to have:

- A plan that fits your unique body, your life, and your strength.
- A team of doctors, friends, family, and community members who show up for you.
- The will to face it one day at a time, even when that day sucks.

Sure, the cancer stage is part of the picture, but it's not the whole story.

The *plan* is.

Advocate for Yourself

In every meeting with every doctor, there will come a moment when you get that funny feeling in your stomach. Maybe it's a quiet nudge. Perhaps it's a visceral reaction to something the doctor said.

This is the moment you step in—for *you.*

In that moment, you have to speak up. Because when it comes to cancer, you can't afford to stay silent.

Doctors must adhere to certain policies and protocols. They map out a timeline based on *their* schedules and patient loads.

But *you* are the one living it. And that means:

- You have the right to ask questions.
- You have the right to understand the information presented.
- You have the right to choose treatments based on your body.
- You have the right to advocate for yourself.
- You have the right to say NO.

How do you advocate for yourself when you feel like you've just landed in another dimension? You're scared, confused, and don't know whether you should laugh or cry at the madness of it all.

You start by asking questions.

Ask Questions

Asking questions will be excruciatingly hard at first. I know— I've been there. You don't know what you don't know, and the terminology surrounding diagnoses and treatment plans is as unfamiliar as another language.

The options feel blurry. The whole thing seems cold and clinical.

Asking questions is how you reclaim your power. It's how you shift the focus from the *label* of your diagnosis to the *strategy* for your treatment. From the *stage* to the *plan*. From *reacting* in fear to *acting* with intention.

This is a mindset shift, and it matters more than anything else right now. Because when you stop seeing yourself as a passive patient and start acting like the decision-maker with your life on the line, everything changes.

You move forward with clarity and strength.

For doctors, it's all very formulaic: If the patient presents with ABC, then we begin treatment XYZ. That's the protocol. It's the textbook approach and the standard of care.

I'm not trying to be critical. It's a necessary approach, especially when there is an overabundance of patients and too few doctors.

But here's the thing: You're not a textbook. You're a person.

- What if XYZ isn't right for *your* body?
- What if there's an alternative treatment, a clinical trial, or a more precise option?
- What about the *why* behind the treatment?
- What about doing testing *before* treating—not just scans, but genetic markers, lifestyle factors, and second opinions?

Too often, patients are expected to sit quietly and comply; to accept a plan without conversation or information. But "standard of care" doesn't mean "one-size-fits-all."

You deserve more than a protocol.

You deserve a plan tailored to you, with room for curiosity and courage, and most of all, a chance to challenge the status quo.

13 Questions Every Cancer Patient Should Ask Their Doctor

When you're hit with the diagnosis, you're flooded with appointments, words you've never heard in your life, and lots of decisions. It's like being shoved into the Tilt-A-Whirl, strapped in, and not being allowed to get off. It's easy to feel like you've lost control.

That's why asking questions is essential. It helps you take back control of your cancer care. You are worthy of a plan that fits you, not just the typical protocol. Asking questions helps you understand your diagnosis, treatment options, risks, and outcomes.

The following are the exact questions I asked in my first appointment. Feel free to add more or delete the ones that don't apply. I want you to have an agenda to use as a guide; a place to start.

Take this agenda with you to your appointment, and bring a trusted friend or family member. You'll need another set of ears to catch all the details or record the meeting for you, if possible.

Be sure to ask the doctor to explain everything in simple terms. Don't worry about sounding dumb. You're not a medical student taking a pop quiz. This is your life, and you need to know everything about this illness that's trying to rob you of it.

1. Can you explain my diagnosis in plain language? You need to understand what you're dealing with, without the medical jargon.

2. What stage is it, and what does that mean for me? Ask how the stage affects your prognosis, but don't let it define your mindset.

3. What are my treatment options, and why are you recommending this one?

   There may be more than one path. You should know the reasoning behind this one. For example, if you choose to use the chemo cap, a device to help reduce hair loss during chemotherapy, you have to know if your chemotherapy regimen supports it. Sadly, the capping didn't work for me, but it was worth a try.

4. When does treatment begin? Before or after surgery? Knowing the timeline helps you put it all in perspective and make plans.

5. What are the goals of the treatment? Remission, control, relief, or prolong your life? This helps align your expectations.

6. Are there any clinical trials or alternative treatments available to me? Don't miss out on emerging therapies or cutting-edge options.

7. What are the potential side effects of this treatment, and how will we manage them?

8. How will your quality of life change? This is about more than just survival.

9. Can I get a second opinion? Will that delay treatment? A good doctor will support and possibly encourage second opinions.

10. What tests or scans will I need before starting treatment? Additional testing can lead to more precise and personalized care.

11. How will this impact my daily life? Work, fertility, finances? You're a whole person, a human whose life outside of treatment matters.

12. What happens if this treatment doesn't work? What's next? Knowing the backup plan gives you peace of mind and a sense of control.

13. Can I add an alternative doctor, like a naturopath, to my care team? Remember, the goal is to get the very best care available. Sometimes that means bringing in other perspectives.

After the appointment, review your notes while they're still fresh in your mind. Discuss your options with your support system and decide if you'll get a second opinion. Take the time you need to process everything you just heard.

You don't need to know everything. You only need to know enough to ask the right questions and understand how to move forward with clarity. This is a leadership mindset, and it is empowerment at its finest.

Write Stuff Down: Low-Tech Is Best

When you walk into an appointment with a list of questions, the whole experience changes. Because I came prepared with my list and a simple printed calendar, I left every meeting more fulfilled, more informed, and less overwhelmed.

It gave me a place to write down terminology I didn't know, and provided me with the opportunity to pause and ask the doctor to repeat or explain anything I didn't understand. I kept track of my appointments, medications, and what I needed to follow up on later so nothing fell through the cracks. It was very old school—just pen and paper—but it worked.

I didn't need a fancy app. I needed focus and clarity. Writing things down gave me a sense of control in a situation where I felt like I was gasping for air.

If you can, bring someone with you to be your second set of ears. But always, always take notes. You're not just the patient anymore; you're the one in charge of this project, and this is your data.

Bring Backup: But Make Sure They're Vetted

Maybe you don't have an assertive, self-assured personality like me. Perhaps you don't feel comfortable taking control of meetings. That's okay! You can bring someone with you to help you through the process.

You're in shock, scared, and maybe angry. It's so hard to process the life-altering ticker tape of word vomit being projected at you, much less know what questions to ask. The last thing you need is to walk out of the meeting and not know which way to turn or what to do next.

At first, I brought my husband with me to take notes and listen. But looking back, I think I was always going to be the one best equipped for that role, given my need for control and how I process information, but that's me. He had other strengths that I leaned on throughout my treatments.

You might bring a family member or a good friend. There are even advocacy groups that can help. Your doctor will probably give you pamphlets on these, but you can also find them online.

Check with your hospital to see if they offer any support programs. The American or the Canadian Cancer Society and the National Coalition for Cancer Survivorship Cancer Policy & Advocacy Team also provide information, programs, and support.

Whoever you take with you, make sure they're level-headed and ready to take notes. If you don't have anyone, ask the doctor if you can record the appointment so you can listen to it later.

Write It Out: Sarcasm Welcome

When I began navigating my diagnosis, I went online and searched high and low. Information is power, and I found a lot of it. I uncovered options the doctors didn't tell me. I found articles and advocacy groups, and I found Facebook groups. A lot of it was incredibly helpful. Some…not so much.

One of the things I noticed in some of these groups was that many people were negative. They were about as helpful as a life coach with a hangover. Don't get me wrong. I completely understand where the negativity came from. Of course I did. But I knew I couldn't live there.

Sometimes, The C Club is like high school. There are all types of people. You've got the popular kids, the band geeks, the class clown, and the overachievers.

If I was going to get through this, I couldn't succumb to the naysayers and cynics. It's not that I didn't have my moments. I could throw a pity party like no other, live band and spiked punch included. But I needed something more if I was going to cross the finish line. I needed to be busy. I decided to add a little levity to my armor in the form of snarky sarcasm and brutal honesty.

I started writing "chapters" about my experiences and posting them in Facebook groups. They were raw and real in all their snarky, sarcastic glory, and it was cathartic. It was also my little way of fighting back against the negativity.

Then something surprising happened. Soon, I began to get comments from strangers saying how much they appreciated my stories. It made them laugh as they sipped their morning coffee, inspired them to go to the gym, and helped them feel less alone.

It didn't take long before I was hooked. Every "like" and comment on my post was a dopamine hit straight to my heart. So I kept going. I kept telling my story, sharing the good, the bad, and everything in between.

I never dreamed it would bring me here, writing this book for you. And I did write it for you. The human one. The angry one. The scared one. The one who isn't ready to give up. The one who still has a life to live and no time for BS.

So if you're feeling stuck, try writing. Even if it's just for you. Even if no one else sees it. If writing isn't for you, try singing or dancing. You don't need *Footloose* moves, just move! It feels good to put your emotions somewhere so you can clear your head and keep moving forward.

We Didn't Choose The C Club; It Chose Us

You let go of the door frame and step into the room with trepidation. The meeting is starting. Someone hands you a name sticker to fill out. Hello, I'm __________. Your first impulse is to fill in the blank with "Lost, Fearful, or Sad." You settle on "Numb."

But then someone starts to speak, and you realize you're not alone. There's power in numbers. You're scared, pissed off. I get it. I was there. My first day in The C Club went about as you would expect.

You feel overwhelmed by doctors, decisions, and everyone else's opinions.

Even now, as a cancer thriver, I still look in the mirror and think, "How the hell did this become my life?"

But remember. You get to choose how you fight. You don't have to do it alone. Stick with me. I'm handing you the "playbook" I created from scratch. I pulled from the hours, days, and years I spent calming companies in crisis and navigating emergencies from a laptop at 30,000 feet in the air.

It wasn't easy. Nothing ever is. During my cancer diagnosis and treatment, both of my parents became sick—then they both passed away within six months of each other. Our home was invaded by would-be car thieves wielding tasers and demanding car keys. They didn't get far. (What kind of car thief doesn't know how to drive a stick?)

But I didn't give up. I didn't give in.

It would have been easier if I could have been shipped to an island, the Island of Misfit Cancer Patients, and stayed there for six months while I went through treatment and recovery. You, too, might wish that you could step out of the microcosm of your life. But you can never really step out of the world.

So throughout the pages that follow, you'll learn how to advocate for yourself, plan your appointments, and still have space to fall apart when you need to.

Then, another sliding door will open. And you'll navigate the best you can. But for now, you have us, your fellow C Club members. So take a seat. Pass the snacks. Share your story when you're ready. We saved you a spot at the table.

CHAPTER 3

Contingency Plan— Navigating Common Hurdles

I spent most of my adult life in airports.

Since the age of 27, I've lived more in boarding gates than in only one city. Some people have baristas who know their coffee order—I have concierges in the Air Canada lounge who greet me with a hug and ask how my daughter is doing.

Chicago O'Hare's crew hands me boarding passes and hugs like we're old friends. The LAX troupe greets me with a hug and ensures everyone with me is taken care of. New York's team calls me by my first name and sometimes asks if I want "the usual." I'm still not sure if they mean my usual terminal or the emotional baggage that comes from logging so many frequent flyer miles.

But this flight would be different, although I didn't know it yet.

It was 2019, and it was my last day as interim CEO at True Religion. I was heading home to Toronto for a little rest and to prep for my next role.

I boarded the plane and got settled in, looking forward to spending time with my family. Just a few more hours and I would be home.

The flight was like so many others. It could have been one of a thousand other flights.

But somewhere over the middle of the country, my phone buzzed.

It was a WhatsApp message from my friend. It read, "You need to call me."

My heart froze. I was 30,000 feet in the air, strapped in, and paralyzed.

My husband—my incredible, active, hockey-playing husband—had gone into cardiac arrest while playing the sport he loved.

"Is he dead?" I texted back.

I was still two hours out of Toronto—an interminable amount of time.

I stood up, tears flowing down my face. I needed to find help.

Suddenly, an angel of a flight attendant appeared out of nowhere. She didn't ask questions. She just knelt next to me as I crumpled back into my seat, gently laid her hand over mine, and said, "I've got you."

She sat there while my brain tried to process the unthinkable while my heart shattered. I had no idea if he would survive. (Spoiler: He did. Because he's just as stubborn as I am.)

That flight attendant held me together when I didn't know how to hold myself. And in that moment, I wasn't the fixer or the strategist. I was just a woman with the wind knocked out of her.

For the next two hours, I texted everyone I could think of while the flight attendant sent a notice to the airport. I would need someone to help me get through customs quickly so I could rush to the hospital.

By the time my husband opened his eyes, he was surrounded by a full support team.

That experience taught me a lot. It's just one of the many experiences, both personal and professional, that prepared me for the fight of my life.

Cancer didn't meet me on day one of my fight. It met me on the tail end of a life I'd already fought tooth and nail to build.

It met a woman who built empires while raising a daughter. A woman who never missed a parent-teacher interview or a dance recital, even if I rolled in from the airport with my suitcase in tow.

A woman who had just lost her own sister to this terrible disease. A sister who, at 11 years older, was a mother figure to her. A woman still in so much pain, anger, and frustration over the Canadian COVID-19 restrictions that wouldn't allow her to see her tough, dying sister—when being next to her was all that should have mattered.

A woman who knows how to survive a crisis without smudging her mascara.

Like me, you have experiences to draw from. You'll need to pull from that tank.

Because cancer doesn't show up when it's convenient. You might be in the middle of a family crisis. Or riding high, enjoying life. That's just how it is. It comes out of nowhere, crashing like a wrecking ball into your carefully built walls. The resulting chaos is a series of hurdles, some obvious and some hidden, that you must navigate to move forward.

In this chapter, I'll share a few of my experiences about how I navigated the most common hurdles you might face at this stage, and how you can overcome them. Hurdles like figuring out your first step after the diagnosis, trusting yourself to make the right decisions in a sea of options, and managing other people's emotions and opinions.

So, what happens in that moment when your whole world crashes down? That's where we begin.

Hurdle 1: First Call, It's Cancer.

You heard the words, but they didn't compute.

Cancer? What does that even mean?

Your mind goes fuzzy. You're physically in the room, but you feel like you're a thousand miles away. Adrift.

It's like the doctor is speaking another language. You don't understand what he's saying, and you're not sure if Google

Translate even knows. His voice sounds distorted, like you're underwater.

Your whole world crashes around you. What do you do now? What does this mean?

The only way through this is to come up for air, take a deep breath, and start building a plan.

That's exactly what I did.

I needed something to focus on. Something I could control, even though it felt like I was about to spiral. I picked up the phone and called my family and friends. And then I opened the MyChart patient portal and pored over every result I could find.

Then I got to work.

I built a binder like I'd done a thousand times before, only this time, it wasn't filled with risk assessments and cash flow statements.

This binder was for me, for my biggest project to date, the biggest turnaround I would ever do in my life. It wasn't just any binder—it was a *cancer* binder. I outfitted it with dividers and filled them with notes, printouts, family history, test results, and appointment summaries. It became my DNA portfolio.

I carried it to every appointment in my Birkin bag. It was a ridiculously heavy bag. I bought it on a whim, and I rarely used it because it's so heavy and uncomfortable, kind of like cancer itself. But I hefted it over my wrist and hauled it like it was the last rowboat on a sinking ship.

At each meeting, even if I was sitting on an exam table, I would open my binder, pass a copy of the agenda to every person in the room, put my glasses on, click my pen open, and begin the meeting.

That's what you do.

Because here's what no one tells you: When the news hits and your brain goes blank, the next step is to anchor yourself in action. Pull together the facts. Call your people. Make a plan. Build your binder.

It doesn't have to be perfect. It's okay to feel like you're a little girl teetering in your mom's high heels. Feeling unbalanced is normal. You don't need to solve everything right now. But if you can start with one step, the rest will follow.

You emerge from that underwater sensation, feeling the solidity of the chair beneath you. The room stops spinning. The floor under your feet grounds you. You hear the doctor saying your name.

You look the doctor in the eyes, pull a notebook and pen from your bag, and say, "Can you please repeat that?"

Three Things You Can Do Right Now to Take Control of This Crisis

1. Open Your Chart

Log in to your medical portal and review your results. Print them out and highlight anything you don't understand. Bring those questions to your next appointment. You're building the foundation for your plan, and that starts with knowing what you're dealing with.

2. Tell One Trusted Person

Share the news with at least one trusted person. Someone who can be your anchor. Let them know you don't have all the answers yet, and ask for support. You don't have to navigate this alone.

3. Grab a Binder

Get a binder, dividers, pens, and highlighters. Put everything in one place—test results, appointment notes, questions, to-dos. Call it your cancer binder, your project portfolio, your survival toolkit, whatever helps you feel in control.

Hurdle 2: Boardroom Instincts—Learn to Trust Yourself

The minute you start sharing the news of your diagnosis, the floodgates open.

Everyone has an opinion. Family, friends—even your nail tech. They mean well, but you didn't ask them for it. There's too much information, too many voices, too many choices, and none of it feels simple.

You want to get this right. You have to—your life depends on it. But you're scared and paralyzed with indecision. How do you trust yourself to make the right choices?

Here's what you need to know: no one knows your body and what you can handle better than you do. Yes, you'll need help, but you are now the CEO of your treatment. You are in charge of all final decisions.

When I started treatment, I asked myself, *How would I approach this if it were a company in crisis?*

I did my research, prepared questions in advance, and documented everything. And when something didn't feel right, or if I thought something was missing, I spoke up.

At first, I didn't want to do chemotherapy. I wanted Herceptin, a targeted therapy drug used to treat certain types of breast cancer that are HER2-positive, like mine. It works by blocking the chemical signals that tell cancer cells to grow. By blocking those signals, Herceptin can slow or stop the cancer's growth. It still has its long list of side effects, but nothing like chemo.

But in Canada, they don't just give you Herceptin. I was willing to go to the US to get it, but I also wanted to be sure it was the right treatment. So I asked for a Ki-67 test, which measures how fast cancer cells are dividing. It gives you an idea of how aggressive the tumor is. And it was the test I needed to know if chemotherapy was the best therapy for me.

I told my doctors that I wanted this test. In Canada, they typically don't do it.

They giggled at me a bit, and I got that "aren't you so cute" look, but since I had done my research, and I was educated and calm, they said, "Okay. Fine. We'll do it."

The results of my test came back. The Ki-67 number was so high that I knew chemotherapy was the right protocol for me.

Knowing this gave me the confidence to go into chemotherapy treatment without wondering if I was doing the right thing.

That's what trusting yourself looks like.

You won't magically know all the answers, but if you listen closely, you'll know when something doesn't sit right with you, and you'll have the courage to speak up. The lesson is this: trust your gut, be clear about what you want, and stay calm.

Three Things You Can Do Right Now to Manage the Outcomes

1. Get a Second Opinion

If that little voice inside your head is whispering, *This doesn't feel right*, get a second opinion. Doctors don't know everything, and it's not disrespectful to ask for another opinion. It's smart. Even though I believe in the power of Western medicine, I spoke to a cancer naturopath to get a different perspective. This is your life, your body, and you're allowed to press pause and say, "I need more information."

2. Do Your Research

The internet is a blessing and a curse. You can find answers to just about anything. But you must choose your sources wisely. Make sure your research comes from reputable medical sources. Ask your doctors for recommendations on where to find the best information. I asked my pharmacist to check all of the vitamins and supplements that my cancer naturopath suggested to make sure there were no contraindications.

3. Keep a Decision Log

Write down what choice you made and why. When brain fog rolls in (and it will), this gives you something solid to come back to. It also helps your family understand your wishes.

Hurdle 3: Agenda Topic—Emotional Labor

Navigating your diagnosis is hard enough without also managing other people's discomfort.

You might worry that people will pity you. Or treat you like you're fragile. Or disappear because they don't know what to say. And maybe you don't even want to tell them because explaining it for the millionth time is exhausting.

I've been there. Bracing for the moment that they uttered the words, "I'm so sorry."

I've heard it more times than I can count. In grocery store aisles, in hospital waiting rooms, in text messages that start with "Hey, just heard…" and fizzle into an awkward silence even through the screen. The phrase floats toward me with a mix of sincerity, panic, and something else I couldn't name at first.

Until I could.

Gratitude. The subtext was: *I'm glad it's not me.*

And somehow, every time they say sorry, I end up backpedaling.

"Oh, no. It's okay. No need to be sorry."

"Really, I'm fine. Everything's fine."

Which is wild because I've lost both my parents, my breasts, my ovaries, my hair, my eyebrows, my eyelashes, my sense of taste, and any illusion of control I ever had. And I'm the one trying to make *them* feel better?

I've become the grief concierge, handing out warm towels and herbal tea while someone awkwardly whispers, "I just can't imagine."

No, you can't. Honestly, I don't want you to. But please, stop apologizing like you caused it, or worse, like it's a burden for you to hear about it.

Sometimes their "sorry" isn't about compassion. It's about self-protection. Because my losses crack open the door to a truth most people spend their entire lives trying to keep shut: This could happen to anyone. *This could happen to me.*

I saw their eyes dart, and heard their voices get small. And I wanted to shake them. Not out of anger, but out of some fierce hope that maybe we could end this ridiculous social dance.

Side note: Let's stop the "I'm sorry" and "it's okay" tango that leaves both parties feeling like awkward teenagers on the dance floor. Instead, say something like, "Thank you for trusting me with what you're going through. What can I do for you?" or "I can imagine you're scared, and I am here to support you in whatever feels right. I'll bring dinner for you tomorrow."

Eventually, something shifted. My identity changed. I didn't always have the emotional bandwidth to manage others' feelings *and* my own cancer treatment.

I wanted to set an automated Out of Office reply with no end date. I wanted to throw a good old-fashioned pity party—for one.

I realized I didn't always have to be responsive. I could delegate that task. As I navigated other people's reactions, I became more honest with myself.

In a sense, I lost my "socially acceptable" filter. If I wasn't okay, I didn't have to pretend I was just so others could feel better about their role in this story—my story.

And you know what? Once I stopped performing for other people's comfort, I had more energy to actually survive this thing.

You can't control what others think or say. You have to listen to your instincts and do what's best for you.

One way I honored my own instincts was on a family trip to California. I woke up one day and said to my husband, "I'm going home. I'm done." Neither my husband nor daughter wanted me to go home alone, but I wanted to; I needed to.

They could have tried to talk me out of it. But I knew I had to go. I let them know how I felt and to their credit, they were okay with it. It's a good thing because their return flight was canceled, and I might have missed my chemo appointment.

So if you're in the thick of this, stop tiptoeing around people's feelings. Stop worrying about them. It's your turn to stand in the spotlight.

Three Things You Can Do Right Now to Deflect Emotional Arrows

1. Be Open and Honest

Say what you need to say. If you don't want to go out to dinner, say no thanks. Let people surprise you with their response. Or not. Either way, don't shape-shift to make them comfortable. Preserve your energy.

2. Set Boundaries

It's okay to put up the Do Not Disturb sign. Not everyone gets full access to you. If you want to leave the party early, leave. No apologies necessary. The best thing I did when I was diagnosed was to write a text message to send out to everyone. That way, I wouldn't be overwhelmed by having to repeat the story over and over. It was a way to conserve my energy by setting a simple boundary.

3. Work on Your Mindset

The thing about being an ambitious, highly motivated president is that you think you can do it all, all the time. But this diagnosis doesn't just change your body. It changes your sense of identity and your relationships. If you're used to being in control of everything and everyone, be kind to yourself. It's okay to let go of the people in your life who bring you down, and welcome the ones who care about you. See this as an opportunity to enrich your life.

Bringing the CEO Energy to Navigate Hurdles

Getting through these first hurdles is no small feat. By now, you've faced some of the hardest moments you never thought would happen. Dealing with these hurdles gives you the confidence to keep going and tackle whatever comes next. If you're here, reading this, you're already doing better than you think.

You've got your bag packed with your binder and a rainbow of highlighters. You've got your list of questions and maybe even given yourself a pep talk in the bathroom mirror. That's an excellent start.

But as you're about to find out, if you haven't figured it out already, a diagnosis like cancer turns you into something you never expected to be: a full-time patient advocate. Plus, *you're* the patient. If you don't speak up and stay on top of your care, no one else will do it for you.

So, how do you do that when you're overwhelmed and unsure?

That's what we'll tackle next.

CHAPTER 4

Power Moves

Being a "good patient" isn't enough; you also have to be smart. That might sound harsh, especially when you're already overwhelmed and exhausted. As I navigated my way through appointments, scans, and treatments, I noticed that the people who have the best outcomes aren't necessarily the ones with the best doctors or who go to the most modern treatment centers.

They're the ones who check their fear at the door and enter appointments with a calm demeanor, prepared to have a practical, matter-of-fact discussion. They're not afraid to speak up. They know what they want from each appointment, so they ask questions and usually get more time and attention from their care team.

Of course, no one is perfect. This is a bumpy ride, and the turbulence can get gnarly. So take time to breathe deeply, lean on your support team, and face the chaos with calm authority and curiosity.

This chapter will cover five actions that I call your Power Moves. These Power Moves aren't magic or overly complicated, but they are incredibly effective because they put you at the head of the table. I've used each one myself, and I've seen the difference they make.

If you want to feel less overwhelmed, more prepared, and more respected in every appointment you walk into, this is where you start.

Let's walk through each Power Move, and I'll show you how to make them work for you.

Power Move #1: Stay Calm and Pragmatic

I love to go hiking. I've hiked all over Arizona, Utah, and Canada in some of the most beautiful places you can imagine.

When you're hiking, there are certain things you do so that you can enjoy the trail and make it home safely: carry food and water, dress for the weather, and know where you're going. But sometimes, people still get lost. They veer off the trail, run out of daylight, or get separated from their group. In most cases, lost hikers are found within a day, but sometimes, tragically, they're not found in time.

One of the main characteristics of a survivor is their mental state. People who stay positive, remain calm, and make deliberate, thoughtful decisions are far more likely to be rescued. Those who panic and give in to despair tend to make poor decisions, which makes it harder for search and rescue teams to find them.

The same is true each time you step into a meeting with your care team. When you stay calm and ask deliberate, thoughtful questions, you get better results. When you panic and unleash all of your pent-up emotions on the medical staff, it makes it harder for them to help you.

Lead With Calm, Even When You Don't Feel It

At each meeting, I was always polite. Every. Single. Time. No matter what type of medically-induced chemical warfare was raging inside me. I would walk into the clinic and say, "Hi, I'm Farla, and I'm accompanied by so-and-so" (whoever won the *Hunger Games* to escort me that day). I led with calm, respectful energy that made it easier for the team to help me—to *want* to help me.

It's funny to read my reports afterward because they all begin with, "Farla is a 51-year-old, very pleasant young woman accompanied by…" And it's, frankly, hilarious because often, inside, I was definitely *not* pleasant. I was exhausted, inflamed, and extremely irritated with my aching knees that clicked like tap shoes in a Broadway audition.

But I didn't show up to vent and complain. I showed up to get what I needed. And the only way to do that was to be cool, calm, and collected.

Calmness Is a Strategy

Staying calm and pragmatic does not mean you have to suppress all of your emotions. You can be emotional and also direct. You can negotiate and debate. It's all about pushing for what you need while keeping your eye on the target.

Maybe you want an updated scan, a better treatment option, or a different drug. Or maybe you ask for clarity on test results, a referral to a specialist, or information on test groups. Having a plan and doing your research gives you the confidence to ask for what you want.

Bring the Receipts

I always brought receipts. Always.

I had (still have) a spreadsheet that tracked every symptom and every reaction beginning from the very first day I started chemo. I called it "Side Effects," and I logged every chemo side effect from nausea and night sweats to constipation and mouth sores. Oh yeah, fun times. I also tracked the type of workout I did each day: boxing, tennis, weights, and walking. I wrote "NA" when the workout didn't happen because sometimes I was just too sick and too tired.

Having this information ready for my doctor made it easier to have a meaningful conversation and get the answers I needed. It meant they didn't have to spend time playing twenty questions while I tried to remember everything that had happened since they saw me last. I became a real person they could collaborate with. They learned my style, that I would push back when I needed to, and they respected me for that.

Doctors Are People Too

You have to remember that doctors are only human. They're inundated with patients and timelines, and they've heard it all before. Their attitude can become short if they've dealt with ten patients before you who zapped their energy. The best thing you can do for yourself, and for them, is to remove as many emotions as you can from the situation and approach them with a calm and practical attitude.

Bonus: Wig Tossing Fantasy

But just for fun, I imagined the alternate reality version of myself, the one who did *not* stay calm.

That report might have read: "Patient arrived unaccompanied, shrieking profanities, ripped off her wig mid check-in, threw her medication bottle like a grenade, and began pointing to various body parts, screaming, 'THESE ARE ALL AFFECTED!' before collapsing onto the scale. Vitals taken amid chaos."

Honestly, I'd kind of respect that version of me. Wigless, fearless, loud, and still probably wearing something cute. But no. I kept it classy. I smiled and said, "Thank you." I'd laugh gently when I'm told my knees are stiff again. Even though I'm surviving on a drug that makes me feel like I've been personally cursed by a Greek god, I'm always polite.

That's what you do. Being pleasant is your superpower, and that's your first move.

Power Move #2: Do Your Research

By going into each appointment prepared, with a balanced approach and research data and questions in hand, I showed my doctors that I meant business. They learned that they could treat me as a partner in my care rather than just another patient with a number and a chip on her shoulder.

If you want to get the best care and treatment you can, not just the standard protocol, you have to do your research. I can't emphasize this enough. I know it feels overwhelming and exhausting, but you have to know everything you possibly can about your type of cancer, or whatever disease or illness you're dealing with, if you want to get the best treatment options available. Even if you believe what your doctors are saying is correct, being educated helps you have better conversations.

No one is going to do this for you. You have to follow every lead, dive down every rabbit hole, and leave no stone unturned.

Don't try to absorb everything at once. There's no way you'll remember everything you learn, especially after the brain fog rolls in. You just need to learn enough to ask smart questions and understand the answers.

Where to Look

I researched the web up and down, backward and forward, until my eyes were bloodshot and my fingers ached. My search terms read like a medical student's textbook:

- Breast cancer (of course)
- Types of breast cancer
- HER2-positive
- Invasive ductal carcinoma

I searched in North America first and then went worldwide, bookmarking every credible source I could find. I started with the Mayo Clinic, Canadian Cancer Society, and Breast Cancer Now (UK).

Johns Hopkins Medicine and the Cleveland Clinic were next on my list. I reached out to them to gain more insight into my diagnosis and understand the treatment options. I read articles from *Scientific American*. I talked to friends and family members with similar diagnoses.

Then, there's YouTube; you'd be surprised at what you can find. I searched "breast cancer stories" and found patient vlogs that were super helpful and relatable because they were real patients, just like me. I tried to find videos on treatments that I was about to go through, so I would know what to expect. I was on a mission to find everything I could about my cancer and anyone who had something even remotely similar.

Finally, I hit up Amazon like I was on a shopping spree at Chanel. I looked at books about starving cancer, eating to beat disease, and foods that fight cancer. I bought books about people who had cancer and how they dealt with it.

I found stories of women who had been through the journey I was about to embark on, and within these stories, I found strength. Some told of finding a lump, calling their doctor, but then not being able to get an appointment for months. In those cases, the women told of how they found ways of getting around the roadblocks, like asking their general practitioner for scans and MRIs, and how they asked for tests, treatments, or surgeries that "weren't typically done" and still got them. That's the kind of CEO energy I want you to have too.

Those stories resonated with me because of my high-risk situation. If there was any chance the cancer would come back in another body part, I wanted it removed—as long as I didn't need it to live.

Western Medicine vs. Naturopathic Medicine

I believe in Western medicine. It saved my life. But I also hired a naturopath to learn more. He pushed me to do additional screening and testing that isn't normally done, specifically within Canada. To be certain these methods were working well together, I always checked any supplements my naturopath doctor suggested with the pharmaceutical team and my oncologist. His perspective gave me a fuller picture of cancer, and its impact on my body.

When you're dealing with a cancer diagnosis, or any chronic or life-threatening illness, you're not limited to one path. Sure, let science take the lead, but don't be afraid to ask questions and explore every option available. At the end of the day, time is all you have, so make the best of it by looking at it from every perspective.

The Midpoint Scan That Gave Me Hope

Here's how doing my research and asking the right questions paid off. The protocol for my chemotherapy plan was six rounds, and then they'd do a scan at the end to see if it worked. Well, that didn't sit well with me. After round three, I asked my oncologist for a scan to see if the chemotherapy was working. If it wasn't, what's the point of continuing down that path?

I did my homework, I made my case, and I got my midpoint scan.

The scan showed that the treatment was working! That moment gave me the hope I needed to strut into rounds four, five, and six wearing designer shoes and an Hermès silk scarf, knowing

I wasn't just enduring these horrific side effects for nothing. I was making progress. Those results were the kind of clarity I needed.

It's Okay If You Don't Know Everything

No matter how many hours you spend researching websites, reading articles, and attending seminars, you won't find all the answers. Do what you can, when you can. I watched YouTube between appointments. I listened to podcasts on the days I had little energy to do much else. I researched one thing at a time, based on what was coming up next in my treatment.

You don't have to know everything; you just need to know enough to make educated decisions and be taken seriously by your care team. So take notes, ask questions, and push back (nicely and politely) when you need to. This is your life. You're allowed to show up and be your own champion.

Power Move #3: Bring an Agenda

Now that you've found your inner calm and done your research, you're ready to walk into your next appointment with a clear objective. The topic of this meeting is your body and its current state of disarray. Your objective is to find out what the next step or treatment is, how it will affect you, and what the desired outcome is.

I didn't want to waste anyone's time, least of all mine. So I made it easy for my care team to help me and get the answers I needed. When you're prepared, you don't have to wait for the doctor to ask questions; you've brought your own.

Make Your Doctor's Job Easier

You might think, "Isn't it *their* job to ask *me* questions?" Sure. But they're juggling dozens of patients with multiple treatment plans. Plus, they're human. They get tired and don't have the mental capacity to always remember what happened at your last visit.

So I gave them a cheat sheet.

Before every single appointment, I prepared an agenda. It wasn't anything fancy, although it can be, if you want. It was a Word document simply titled "Cancer Agenda," in Times New Roman, with the date and the doctor's name at the top. I had a lot of appointments, so I made a lot of agendas! It's safe to say that Word Docs and I became very good friends.

My agenda included the following:

- A rundown of symptoms
- Treatment side effects
- Allergic reactions
- New issues that have popped up since our last meeting

It included questions about the treatment and drug options. It included "pros and cons" and the benefits of different types of surgeries. I often included any statistics and data I had uncovered. For instance, item ten on one agenda with my oncologist reads:

Benefits of Hysterectomy, i.e., Prophylactic Ovary Removal:

Studies show that people who have a hysterectomy (uterus and ovaries) have a 30% increased survival rate since it removes the source of estrogen in the first place. Good idea?

No, I wasn't being *extra*. Not this time. My agendas were efficient because if my doctor walked into the room already briefed, the conversation got down to business, and the results got better.

Pretty Is As Pretty Does

You can make your agenda look pretty and professional, or you can just keep it simple. After all, you're not entering it in a design contest. I kept it simple because by the time the meeting was over, I had covered it with serial killer handwriting scribbled in both margins with words crawling at different angles across the flipside. It was a cipher, but I had the answer key.

Here's what matters:

- Bring a list of relevant questions.
- Bring a timeline of what's changed since your last visit.
- Give a copy to the nurse before the doctor walks in.
- Highlight what you need: more testing, a medication change, a referral, a second opinion.

Simple is an underrated strategy. But it sends a clear message: I'm here to collaborate with you on my treatment.

Real Outcomes

When you show up ready to get down to business, your doctor doesn't have to waste precious time flipping through your file. All of the relevant information is already in their hands, and with a quick look, they can ask better questions. Which often means better options for you.

During one appointment, because I had listed a new set of side effects (mouth sores, ugh!) along with a timeline of when they occurred, the doctor was able to quickly recommend a solution. I was offered a prescription for "magic mouthwash." Not joking. But that's the kind of conversation you can expect when you come prepared. This one shift made appointments more tolerable, plus, I would not have had that result if I had waited to be asked.

Navigating your treatment is your full-time job now, so why not make it as easy as possible? Create a simple agenda using your favorite software or program. Or go old school and keep it all in a spiral notebook. It doesn't matter what you use, as long as you use something.

Make sure you have the date, name of the doctor, reason for the appointment, and plenty of space for questions, answers, medications, and results. If it helps, we've included a sample template in the appendix to get you started. Use it, modify it, do whatever you need to do to make it relevant to you, just make sure you never walk into your appointments empty-handed—this little secret weapon holds a lot of power.

Power Move #4: Build Your Inner Circle

Even though it felt like I was a one-woman band—lead singer, guitarist, drummer, and backup singer all-in-one—cancer isn't a solo artist gig. It's a full-time job, and you are going to need a full band, if not a full orchestra, to navigate this world tour.

The kind of support you'll need will change depending on where you are in your treatment and recovery process. Some days, you may only need an acoustic guitarist, someone who can accompany you to appointments. Other days, you'll need a driver, a grocery shopper, a personal chef, a chemo buddy, and someone to pick up your prescriptions when you're too wiped out to move. Sometimes you'll just need a dog, AKA the band mascot. (More on that in a minute.)

Whatever stage you're on, you don't have to go it alone, and you shouldn't try to.

My Chemo Crew

I wore designer running shoes to my first chemo treatment. Why? Because I could. I needed to prove to myself that I was still me and hadn't waved the white flag to surrender to this thing.

I also brought snacks, a clipboard, and a planner. The nurse looked at me like I'd wandered into the wrong room.

"You sure you're here for chemo?"

"Yup," I said, clicking my pen. "And I have some notes."

Let me tell you something about chemo. It doesn't care about your outfits, or your accomplishments, or how well you planned your week.

It comes for you. And it strips you, layer by layer, until you're raw, real, and face-to-face with yourself. But that day, I held the line. I sat in that chair, designer kicks on, chin up, talking strategy and dinner plans and to-do lists. Because I was still me.

That day, I decided if this cancer wanted to try me, I'd show it who it was dealing with. From then on, I had a group of friends who came with me to chemo. I called them my Chemo Crew.

I created a sign-up sheet so people could pick the days they wanted to come. Everyone was committed. I had an agenda (of course I did), so they knew who was picking up my meds, who was running errands, and who was bringing the snacks.

They saw me at my most emotionally raw and drained state, chemo cap on, drugs mainlining into my port, yet it was incredible because I got to hang out with my girlfriends. It was a celebration, a food fest, and an '80s dance party, even if I could barely "bust a move" from my chemo lounge chair.

Patient Plus Band Manager

You're not just the patient; you're also the point person, and you need backup. It's really hard to accept help when you're used to doing it all yourself, but a good CEO or president knows how to delegate. And that's what I did.

I had lots of help. I had people who drove me to appointments, picked up groceries, and some who would just sit and keep me company. One girlfriend even let me borrow her dog for a week. I don't own a dog, but I love them, and it was so wonderful she did that for me. If owning a pet is too overwhelming, check your local shelter to see if they offer a Doggy Day Out. If you're a cat person, search "cat café" in your area to find places where you can visit cats.

The great thing about having a good support system is that the team also protects your primary caregiver from getting burned out. Thanks to my friends, my husband was able to get some rest so he could take better care of me.

Choose Your Crew With Care

When my friends asked what they could do to help, I told them I would love for them to come to chemo with me, but only if they were okay with it. Some people aren't up for something like that, and I understood. So I offered other ways they could help, and I let go of any expectations.

Your energy is precious. You need people who are willing to show up and dance with you in the infusion room or belt out "Eye of the Tiger" while driving you to your next appointment. Be grateful for the ones who show up, and don't worry about the others. If all they can muster is to send you a funny meme, at least they're trying. Chalk it up to cancer ghosting. That's when a friend or loved one becomes distant or disappears entirely. Sometimes it's a sign of emotional immaturity on their part. Or, it could mean that seeing you in pain is bringing up a traumatic event in their life that they've worked hard to bury. Either way, save your energy for your recovery.

Extra Support

As I progressed through my treatment, I hired a third-party service called CTOAM, Cancer Treatment Options & Management Inc.

They weren't part of my hospital team; they were an external group of experts who offered oncology services. I wanted to double-check that I was still on the right treatment path, and they helped me with additional testing and screening. It was part of my "leave no stone unturned" approach.

As you assemble your support system, just know that it doesn't have to consist entirely of close friends and family. It can include professionals, community groups, Facebook groups, or even someone you meet in the waiting room at your next appointment.

You don't have to set up your support system overnight, and you don't have to host a rad chemo party if that's not your style. Trust your judgement, stand in your power, and let people in when you're ready.

Power Move 5: Handle the Paperwork

Let's talk about the one thing no one wants to talk about: What happens *if*.

What happens if you don't get better?

What happens if the treatment doesn't work?

What happens if your time is shorter than you hoped?

I didn't want to think about that either. But I didn't want my family to have to worry about my final wishes when all they should be doing is grieving. So, true to form, I made a list to get my affairs in order, and I got busy chipping away at it. Mine looked something like this:

- Last Will and Testament
- Power of attorney for property and finances
- Power of attorney for personal care
- Advance Care Directive for end-of-life wishes

- Passwords, logins, and digital access
- Personal legacy (life stories and autobiographical information)

This isn't an exhaustive list—we'll go into more detail later when I share my Healing Rebel Protocol. But this will give you a place to start with the items that will have the biggest impact on you and your loved ones. I didn't want anyone to have to guess what I wanted. This was about protecting my identity and how I showed up in the world, even after I was gone. Yes, it feels morbid, but you have to do it. You have to have a plan in place because, at the very least, it will give you peace of mind knowing that you've done everything you could.

And then, you get back to the business of fighting.

CHAPTER 5

Hope Is Not a Strategy

You can read everything there is to know about your illness and diagnosis, but if you don't put those Power Moves into play, then everything I've shared with you so far doesn't matter.

If you don't show up ready to take control of your care, the system will take control for you. The system is not built to prioritize your goals; it's built to manage patients by following protocols. That means that if you want something different, if you want a test or medication that doesn't follow protocol, you have to push for it.

The healthcare system doesn't give you what you deserve. It gives you what you fight for. You have more control than you think, but only if you claim it. Will you always get what you want? Probably not. Will you make choices you later regret? Absolutely. I did.

But I never regretted asking the questions, seeking alternative perspectives, and pushing my doctors to think outside the box.

What Happens When You're Not Informed

Imagine running a company where you never review the financials and never question your advisers. You just nod, sign the paperwork, and hope for the best.

You probably wouldn't be running the company for long with that type of thoughtless approach to leadership. Yet that's exactly how many people approach their health care and treatment.

They hand the decisions over to the doctors because they're the experts, right? But they don't know your body like you do. They don't know your family history, your values, your priorities, or your fears.

If you don't know your options, you might be talked into a course of treatment that doesn't align with your goals. You might not get certain tests, like the Ki-67 test I asked for, because you didn't know about them, or even know that you could request additional tests. You might nod along, sign the paperwork, and hope for the best.

Without your input, doctors will do what they're trained to do: follow standard procedures. Standard procedures streamline the care and treatment of patients. But in most cases, the standard procedure is not good enough. It's not that doctors don't want to give their patients the best care possible. It's that doctors often don't have time to keep up-to-date with emerging treatment options. That's where you come in.

Don't leave critical decisions in someone else's hands. You are unique. You come with one-of-a-kind DNA. Your care should be tailored to you through targeted therapies. Your protocol should be personalized to you, and this is accomplished by advocating for yourself.

Let me show you what I mean.

My Double Mastectomy Fight

When I was diagnosed with a triple positive breast cancer—Stage 2B invasive ductal carcinoma, HER2-positive—I had a choice: lumpectomy or mastectomy. The standard protocol would have suggested lumpectomy. It's less invasive, has a quicker recovery time, and is considered to be an effective treatment.

I did my research and reached out to everyone I could think of who had breast cancer. What I found was that in many of the women I talked to, the cancer returned—sometimes two or three times. The common denominator in those whose cancer returned was that they did not opt for a double mastectomy.

I also had a family history that was basically a gigantic red flag waving over my life. My mother, my sister, my grandmother, and my aunt all had breast cancer. I knew what the fight entailed: chemotherapy, hair loss, fatigue. If I chose to do a lumpectomy, there was a high likelihood that the cancer would return. If I opted for a single mastectomy, there was a high likelihood that the cancer would return. I certainly didn't want to have to go through months of debilitating treatments a second or third time.

So I said to my surgeon, "I want to do a double mastectomy."

And the room got quiet.

My oncologist supported me in this decision. My radiologist said that my breasts were so dense that she wouldn't even debate the question; she would do it. But my surgeon pushed back. She didn't want to remove healthy breasts and cited a long list of complications and risks associated with the surgery and reconstruction. She told me that I didn't need to go that far.

Remember when I said that no one knows your body like you do? No one knows your family history, your fears, your resilience.

Well, that surgeon didn't know me. She didn't know how far I would go.

I pretty much lost it. Right then and there. This was probably the only time during my entire treatment process that I did *not* stay calm for my doctors.

What you have to understand is that I was in a very vulnerable state. At that very moment, my mother was in an operating room six hours away in Montreal, undergoing brain surgery to remove a cancerous tumor. This was her *third time* fighting— she had already beaten it twice. Plus, I had lost my sister to cancer. I was not taking any chances.

I looked at the surgeon and said, "I am like a ticking time bomb. We're going to take out both my breasts. That's what we're doing. Just give me the papers."

Eventually, she got it. After that, we had a better conversation and talked about things like nipple preservation, reconstruction, and risks. But none of that would have happened if I hadn't known what I wanted—what I *needed*—and fought for it.

Know When to Push, Know When to Let Go

There's a difference between being pushy and being informed.

I actually pushed very hard for radiation. But my cancer was not in the lymph nodes, so my team said no. I knew I was being a little crazy. I wanted that extra layer of protection I thought would come from radiation treatment. But once I had a frank conversation with my team, walking through the data and the risks, I backed off.

Being educated helped me know when to stop pushing and let it go.

You don't have to win every debate. That's not what this is about, but you do have to show up ready to have the debate in the first place.

Regrets That Still Haunt Me

Even with all the research I did, the self-advocacy, and the CEO energy, I still live with two big regrets; two moments when I either made the "wrong" choice or didn't act fast enough.

The first one happened when I was 42. A doctor from the high-risk program I was in recommended I go on tamoxifen, a type of hormone therapy sometimes used to reduce the risk of breast cancer in high-risk individuals. It could have reduced my chances of developing cancer, but it could have also pushed me into early menopause.

At that time, my daughter was 12, and I still hoped to have another child. But I'd had four miscarriages. Deep down, I held onto that small glimmer of hope that I would have another baby. If I chose this drug, that dream would be gone forever. Tamoxifen is not safe to take if you're trying to conceive due to the risk of birth defects. I chose to honor that hope, and I did not take tamoxifen.

If I had gone on tamoxifen when I had the chance, would I have escaped breast cancer? I'll never know. Since I did get breast cancer, was the choice "wrong?" It's easy to look back and say, *I should have chosen differently*. But the truth is, I made the best decision I could at the time. I have to leave it at that.

The second regret happened after my sister was diagnosed with esophageal cancer and then breast cancer. She had been through hell with it and had no choice but to do a single mastectomy.

I contacted my high-risk doctor and asked for more extensive genetic testing. I hadn't been diagnosed yet, and testing revealed that I didn't have the BRCA gene mutation, which would increase my cancer risk. The results also showed that I had no other mutations of consequence.

Due to my high risk, the doctor and I discussed doing a preventive double mastectomy. I brought the topic up due to my fear of getting breast cancer. But the catch was, it would be a long road filled with lots of tests and psychological evaluations. Doctors won't sign off on removing healthy breasts without being sure that it's in the best interest of the patient. I really wanted to do it, and I was gearing up for it, but then my sister got extremely sick. Suddenly, I had other priorities.

So I dropped it.

Here's the crazy part. After watching my mom, my sister, and my aunt suffer from cancer, I thought, "Maybe I'll be the one who doesn't get it. Everyone in the family can't get cancer, right? That's impossible." Maybe I was going to be spared.

But guess what? Hope is not a strategy. I had the chance to increase my odds by going forward with the double mastectomy, but I missed it.

Those are two moments I carry with me. Whenever I have to make a tough decision, I ask myself, *Am I going to regret this?*

This Is Your Call

When I was finally diagnosed, there was no effing way I was not going to fight for anything and everything until I got what I wanted. I pushed for it all. It was hard and confusing at times. Did I second-guess myself? Yes, yes, I did. But I made the decisions, and I owned them.

Even with all of the planning, researching, and education, it comes down to your choice. Remember, you always have a choice. You just have to be as educated as you can and then trust yourself to make the right decisions.

Use the Power Moves you learned in chapter 4 to help you. They are the foundation for self-advocacy and will help you get the best treatment possible. Continue revisiting them and applying them to each new appointment and decision you encounter.

I made the decision very early on that I was going to go to the extreme to take out anything and everything that I no longer needed—breasts, fallopian tubes, ovaries—to have the best chance that cancer would not come back.

Cancer would never be my weakness; it's my strength.

PART 2

Bringing the CEO Energy

CHAPTER 6

The Healing Rebel— Managing Cancer Like a Consulting Project

I didn't want to "do cancer" the way everyone expected me to. I wasn't going to sit quietly and nod politely while my treatment was laid out and decided for me. I had spent decades running companies, negotiating turnarounds, and building winning strategies—even when the numbers didn't add up. So, no, I wasn't about to be a passive passenger on this ride.

I realized I already had what I needed. I had been preparing my whole life for this, and I didn't even know it. My best chance at beating this thing, this ugly, horrible thing that had already taken my sister, was me.

My experience in the business world was my best survival tool. I became the consulting project, and I hired my CEO brain to solve the problem. I didn't have a team; I was the team. So I called myself the Healing Rebel, suited up in my favorite couture, and got to work.

The Power of a Playbook for Healing

When life throws you into a health crisis, the chaos is overwhelming and relentless. You have appointments, test results, treatments, side effects, decision after decision, not to mention a large dose of fear and uncertainty. Without a system, it's easy to feel crushed by the weight of it all.

That's where a playbook for healing comes in. It's more than just a checklist and schedule. It becomes your guide, your portable command center. It's the engine that keeps everything running and moving forward, even when all you can muster is to move from the bed to the couch. It acts as the filter that prioritizes what matters most. It aligns everyone with the mission: survival.

The Healing Rebel Protocol

When I started treatment, I felt the ground shift beneath me. It was like daily tremors shaking my world. One day I'd feel strong, the next I'd be curled up in bed, wondering if I'd ever feel normal again. My emotions were all over the place, my energy and patience worn thin, and keeping up with my appointments was a full-time job on top of my already full-time job.

I needed a central command center; a protocol to control all the variables and stay on top of the moving parts. Let me be blunt: Winging it in cancer treatment is like showing up to a multimillion-dollar negotiation without doing your homework. You might get lucky. But more than likely, you'll be laughed at and fired on the spot. So I took command in the only way I knew how by using research, spreadsheets, agendas—the things a CEO's dreams are made of!

And that's how the Healing Rebel Protocol was born.

This protocol is the mechanism that makes my entire framework work. It's going to be your blueprint for navigating your illness. From understanding your diagnosis to knowing your treatment plan, it's about commanding your comeback with precision, intention, and with a mindset that says: *I'm running this show.*

The Healing Rebel Protocol is the bridge between feeling like cancer is happening *to* you and taking charge so it happens *with* you. You become an active player, calling shots, making informed decisions, and protecting your energy.

It's a strategic operating system for your health and life, built on the same leadership principles I used in business, but adapted to the reality of a body in a cancer crisis. It gives you control over your choices, allows you to create boundaries, and shows your team of healthcare providers that you are partners in your treatment.

Within this central command mechanism, I've developed a few strategies and mindset shifts that help the Healing Rebel Protocol run smoothly:

- Blue-sky thinking
- Meetings—not appointments
- Owning personal decision
- Assembling a "board of advisers."

Let's get started.

Blue-Sky Thinking

One approach I learned in my years of turning companies around was to stretch my team to hit higher goals. I used a concept called blue-sky thinking. It's a creative brainstorming approach that focuses on generating ideas without limitations or constraints. I would ask my team to expand the possible solutions to the highest level, even if it sounded crazy or unattainable. Once we knew what was possible, we'd bring it back down to the most realistic solutions.

I used this approach with my cancer diagnosis and treatment. I asked myself, "If the sky is the limit, what's possible? What's out there for me?"

Then I brought it back to the realistic options that were available to me based on my particular type of cancer, living in Canada, and funding limitations. My goal was to determine which solutions I would advocate for. I gathered all of this information and identified opportunities for solutions, along with the actions that I would need to take.

This project would be my biggest accomplishment to date. No quarterly earnings or C-suite salaries to save—just my life on the line.

Cancer may have taken my job from me, but that didn't mean I couldn't work. Now, my full-time job was fighting cancer and staying alive. I swapped Fortune 500 boardrooms for oncologist exam rooms. Instead of choosing which company to save next, I was deciding which hospital had the best team for me. Instead of flying business class for corporate turnarounds, I traveled to meetings to save myself.

Meetings, Not Appointments

In the medical world, anytime you meet with a doctor, it's typically called an "appointment." But I called them "meetings." It's a subtle language shift, but words shape how you show up. In this game, showing up like a leader changes everything from mindset to your stature and demeanor. That attitude shift makes a world of difference when it comes to advocating for yourself and being taken seriously by your doctors.

When you attend a meeting, you always have an agenda, data, statistics, and next steps. You never go in blind. Remember those Power Moves from chapter 4? Leading up to each meeting, I did my research and created an agenda. By the time my doctors sat down with me, they had already been briefed on my status and were ready to talk about solutions.

The decision to show up to the doctor's office this way is crucial because when you've got poison running through your body, it tends to wear you down. I felt like I was having an out-of-body experience, and I didn't have the patience that I typically would have to sit in meetings and recall everything that had happened to me since the last meeting. Plus, brain fog had kicked in, so it's likely I would have forgotten.

Knowing this logistical hurdle, I kept a day-to-day summary of my symptoms, any exercise I did, and how I felt in general. It was like creating a report for the board, only this time, my health was the Key Performance Indicator (KPI).

This type of approach left very little room for emotion. I needed solutions, not sympathy. I didn't need to be coddled. Sympathy wasn't going to reduce the nausea or stop my hair loss. Honestly, unless you've gone through this kind of treatment, you really have no idea what it's like. So, to sit with a doctor who hasn't gone through it and try to have a pity party just doesn't work. That's not to say I wouldn't have enjoyed a party, but I needed action. I didn't have a lot of energy to spare, so when I went in prepared, action and solutions were what I got.

Personal Factors in Every Decision

In any cancer treatment plan, the decisions you'll need to make are endless. Decisions like whether your treatment plan will include a mastectomy, lumpectomy, radiation, surgery (or surgeries), chemotherapy, immunotherapy, or a combination of these, plus additional medications. These decisions also factor in whether you are physically, mentally, and financially prepared for the battle.

Your treatment is a very personal decision, and you have to consider all of the individual factors that make you unique, as well as the circumstances that surround the cancer. You have to decide whether you have the right support because you're going to need a lot of it. This is where blue-sky thinking comes in. What are your options? Sit down and brainstorm every possible path, even if it seems unattainable.

Before you can make decisions about your treatment, you need to know why those specific treatment options are being offered in the first place. This all goes back to understanding what type of cancer you have, what stage and grade it is, and what the pathology means. You have to be informed, and you have to know your options.

Behind every decision I made were four guiding questions: two about survival, two about regret.

- Will this give me the strongest chance to stay alive—and stay well?
- Does this protect me from cancer returning or spreading?
- Will I look back and feel proud of this choice, no matter the outcome?
- If I say no, will I carry that decision as a weight or a wound?

Since I was young and healthy when I was diagnosed, I decided to take a very aggressive route. I knew I would be strong enough to handle the treatment. If I had been older or not in the best of health, I would have made a different decision.

When I decided to do a double mastectomy, I looked at it from every angle. I knew the risks of removing my breasts, but I also knew that there was a risk of the cancer returning if I kept them. I had the data. I had the research. That's not to say I wasn't scared. Doubts crept in right up until the day of the surgery. But I kept reminding myself of the data I had collected regarding the reduction of the recurrence rate. That knowledge calmed me and allowed me to move forward. I made an informed decision, and I don't regret it.

Keep in mind that no one's decisions are perfect. You don't have to worry about choosing differently from someone else. Even if you chose the same path, your outcome would be different because you are different. Your path is as unique as you are. The key is to take ownership of your path and make the best decisions you can.

Your Personal Board of Advisers

Building the right team around you is essential to your treatment and your sanity. At first, my husband attended the oncology meetings with me, and it was great to have his support. I wanted him there. I needed him there with me. But I quickly learned that he wasn't going to be able to offer the type of support I needed in those meetings. I needed someone who would speak up, ask questions, take notes, and have my back to push for things I wanted in my treatment.

It's not that he wasn't able to support me. He's very well spoken, smart, and attentive, but it's not in his nature to challenge the doctor's suggestions, whereas I challenged everything. After one meeting, I asked him why he hadn't spoken up. He said that he had never witnessed what he saw that day. He watched me hand out agendas, ask about prescriptions, make new appointments, and basically run the show. He said, "It's like they're working for you."

No matter how strong you are or how well prepared you are for meetings, you *will* need help. You may not have a spouse or partner to lean on as I did. It might be a close friend, family member, or even a volunteer advocate.

You'll need someone to drive you, someone to take notes or record meetings, someone who will ask questions, and others just to be there for you. You'll need help with meals, errands, and housekeeping. Because when the nausea hits, when your brain is filled with fog, and your energy is zapped, you'll have the peace of mind knowing your team is there to carry on. Assembling a winning care team is easier than you think, and I'll show you how to do that in the next chapter.

Owning the Project

Shifting from being a president and CEO to being a patient was a little jarring. I went from corner offices and pencil skirts to hospital rooms and paper gowns. But I refused to leave my leadership skills at the door.

From the very beginning, I knew I wanted to live, and I was going to do everything in my power to give myself more days on this planet with my family. Every choice I made was weighed against the benchmarks about survival and regret that I mentioned earlier.

Taking ownership of your treatment changes the game. It puts you in a position of empowerment. The Healing Rebel Protocol wasn't just about saving my life. It gave my family, friends, and care team a clear way to plug into my treatment and healing plan without me constantly explaining or negotiating. The protocol can do the same thing for you. It will help you make sure everyone knows the plan, your boundaries, and how you measure progress.

Sure, there will be setbacks along your journey, but having a clear path forward provides clarity. It gives you back the energy you desperately need to fight...it is very rewarding. For me, with this protocol, I achieved what I needed to do, and I felt validated with each little win.

Now that we've covered the principles behind the Healing Rebel Protocol, I'll break down exactly how to implement it into your own life. Whether you're dealing with a cancer diagnosis or another life-altering illness, the next chapter will show you how to adapt the protocol to your unique circumstances.

Because the truth is, your comeback doesn't happen by accident. It happens because you tap into your leader mindset and follow the protocol that makes your comeback inevitable.

CHAPTER 7

The Healing Rebel Protocol—Your Playbook for Commanding Your Comeback

When I was first diagnosed, I didn't fully understand the way that cancer would take over my life. I thought I would continue to do the work I loved and fight cancer in my spare time. Obviously, that didn't work out. Fighting cancer was the hardest thing I've ever done, and my post-cancer body still struggles daily.

When I first created the Healing Rebel Protocol, I didn't see it as a neat six-step framework. I was just trying to survive, and the steps fell into place organically as I worked through my diagnosis and treatment.

Of course, I didn't wander into my treatment blind. As the president of a consulting firm whose job it was to restructure companies, it just wasn't in my nature to "go with the flow" on my treatment plan. So I designed a system on the fly and built a structure based on my 30 years of experience.

Essentially, by simply doing what I would normally do in my day-to-day job, I created a playbook that kept me sane in the midst of all of the unknowns. It allowed me to show up as the CEO of my own health and provided an organized framework from which to heal.

In chapter 6, I presented the mindset and principles behind the Healing Rebel Protocol. Now, I'll share with you the exact operating system I implemented during my treatment. Think of it as your playbook, which you can adapt to your own circumstances. Whether you're facing cancer, another health crisis, or any seismic disruption that shakes your world, all you need is a willingness to see yourself as the leader of your own comeback.

This is how I ran cancer like a consulting project. It's how you can take charge of your treatment and healing too.

Step 1: Pause Before You Panic

You've just received the most devastating news: It's cancer. The world tilts. Time stands still. Panic sets in, and your brain revs into overdrive. *What do I do now?* The questions come fast. Fear walks in the door and takes a seat, and it wants answers.

Before you spiral, take a deep breath.

In business turnarounds, I never walked into a failing company and made sweeping changes without first pausing to gather facts. The same applies here. Your first job after hearing the words "you have cancer" is not to sprint into action; it's to stop, take a few breaths, and gather yourself together.

When I got my diagnosis, I wanted answers immediately, just like anyone in this situation would. But I learned that very few cancer decisions can be made in the first 24 to 48 hours. The truth is that the doctors don't even have any answers for you yet. All they know is that it's cancer and whether or not it's invasive. They haven't completed the whole pathology to know what stage or grade it is.

So in those early moments, give yourself permission to pause. Talk to your family, call a trusted friend, or just take a walk. Create the mental space you need to wrap your head around the news and approach it as a strategist would.

Your next appointment with your oncologist may not be for a few weeks, which feels like a torturously long time to wait. It's also possible that the oncologist will want to take another biopsy before you sit down with them to get the details of your diagnosis.

Use that "in limbo" time to start doing your blue-sky thinking, the strategy we talked about in chapter 6. If anything were possible, what outcome would you want? I didn't want to die, and I didn't want the cancer to come back, so I decided to take an aggressive approach.

Sit down and play the "what if" game. Start thinking about what approach you'll take if the diagnosis is not too bad, somewhat bad, or terminal. Of course, there are so many variables that you just don't know, but taking action in some small way helps you feel calm and in control, even if it's just the illusion of control.

Next, gather your family's medical history. The more medical information you have about your parents, grandparents, siblings, aunts, and uncles, the more informed you'll be. If you've had any genetic testing done, assemble those results as well.

Before long, panic will start to wear off, and when you finally meet with your doctor, you'll go in with a more practical mindset, armed with information, and ready to partner with your doctor to make a treatment plan.

Step 2: Assemble Your Executive Board

A good president doesn't run the company alone, so why should you fight for your life alone? In every company I've turned around, success came down to the strength of my team. It's no different with cancer, or any life-altering illness. Your Executive Board, in this case, is made up of your care team, your advocates, and your supporters.

I created an organizational structure that included my professional care teams, like the oncologist and cancer specialists. Then I had what I call my village, which was made up of friends and other support people.

Here's a list of potential Executive Board members:

- Oncologist
- Nutritionist
- Psychiatrist

- Psychologist
- Naturopath
- Pharmacist
- Chiropractor
- Massage therapist
- Heath and fitness instructor
- Family
- Friends

At this point, you might be overwhelmed with the size of your Executive Board, or maybe you're wondering how in the world you're going to pay for all of this. Before you hyperventilate, take a breath while I share some good news with you.

Hospitals often offer free programs that provide phenomenal support through a range of specialized educational courses covering the full spectrum of cancer care, from diagnosis to treatment to celebrating the positive outcomes.

In Canada, I was referred to Wellspring Cancer Support. Through the hospital and Wellspring, I assembled my Executive Board. Most major hospitals have something like Wellspring, and much of it is free. You'll leave your first meetings with dozens of informational pamphlets on how and where to get help. They also offer assistance to the patient's family members. With all of this support, you don't have to be alone.

Assembling this board doesn't happen by accident. You'll need to interview and vet specialists, assign roles, and compile a contact list. For instance, you'll want at least one trusted person who is calm, organized, and supportive to act as your Executive

Assistant. This person will help you coordinate appointments, take notes in meetings, and ask questions when your brain is too foggy.

Keep in mind that your Executive Board doesn't need to be large; you may not need every person from the list above, but it does need to be intentional. Just like in business, having the right people in the right roles helps determine success, so choose people who bring value.

You're only as strong as your team. Handpick your players and don't be afraid to make changes. In my world, and yours, every seat at the table needs to serve a purpose.

Step 3: Conduct a Medical Audit

Before making decisions, you need to gather data. Just like in business, you don't make decisions based on guesswork. You audit before you act. You gather the numbers, the history, the risks, and the opportunities.

When your life is at stake, you do all of that prep work and more. You leave no stone unturned. A medical audit helps you assemble the information you need to make informed decisions. In step 1, we talked about gathering family histories and family medical information. This time, it's all about you.

A medical audit means gathering every piece of data related to your health, diagnosis, and treatment. Let me break it down for you:

Health Care and Treatment Details

- Medication list—All current prescriptions, dosages, schedules, and side effects

- Treatment history—All past medical treatments to include:
  - » Surgeries
  - » Chemotherapy
  - » Radiation
  - » Immunotherapy
  - » Other interventions with dates and outcomes
  - » Doctor's notes and explanations
- Testing
  - » Blood tests
  - » Genetic tests
  - » Scan and biopsy results
  - » Pathology reports
- Allergies and adverse reactions to drugs, foods, or materials (important for future care)
- Research on your type and stage of cancer

Personal Health Tracking

- Nutrition and lifestyle notes: diet plans, exercise routines, sleep tracking
- Symptom diary—daily notes on fatigue, pain, mood, or other changes
- Quality of life measures—self-assessments to track how treatment affects daily living
- Questions for doctors—running list to bring to each appointment

Supportive Care

- Mental health and counseling records: therapy notes, support group participation
- Palliative or supportive care options: pain management, symptom relief strategies, and care available in your region and beyond

Digital copies are great; you'll want to save them in a place where you and family members can easily access them. But the best way to understand the information is to print it out, highlight important pieces, and circle terms you don't know so you can ask questions. If you're missing anything, request copies.

While it's true that your doctor should have all of your information, don't assume they do. Departments don't always talk to each other, and sometimes things get overlooked. You need to be the one holding the complete set of facts.

That's what the medical audit does. It gives you a full picture of where you stand at any given moment—that's powerful. Because once you have the facts, you can make informed decisions instead of operating from assumptions.

If this step feels overwhelming, take a deep breath and focus on one item at a time. Start with one bullet point, like putting together your medication list, and then make a goal to chip away at it a little each day. It doesn't have to be perfect, but the more information you can gather, the better your doctors will be informed and the easier it will be for you to make decisions.

By the time I met with my oncologist to map out a treatment plan, I already knew what plan she would propose. I had watched videos from women with my identical type of cancer and learned about the protocol they used. But even then, I asked questions and pushed back because I wanted to make sure I was getting the best possible options.

I assembled all of my medical audit information into a binder that I took to every meeting. I added all the information I gathered from my research, which included treatment options, statistics on different protocols, and data on medications. I kept spreadsheets with dates, treatments, and side effects. I used a calendar to track medicine and dosages. I compared hospital options and specialists the way I used to compare competitors in an industry. Knowledge became my negotiating power, and I used it many times.

Step 4: Don't Make Major Decisions Alone

In the corporate world, major decisions are never made by one person. They are made with input from the team after analysis and discussion. The same applies here.

Cancer treatment is full of major decisions: surgery or no surgery, chemotherapy or alternative therapies, lumpectomy or mastectomy. These choices carry lifelong consequences, and no one should have to make them alone.

Wait until you've done your research and spoken to your medical team. It's natural to want to go straight to "Dr. Google." But before you spiral from search results that warn of risk factors and death statistics, remember that you're just there to gather facts and data. Your goal is to read and learn about your type of cancer or illness so that you can understand it. You're not trying to find a solution. That comes later.

When the doctor lays out a plan, you'll be armed with the knowledge to ask questions and have an informed conversation about the treatment and whether there are additional tests you might want, like I did when I asked for the Ki-67 test to determine whether chemotherapy was the right course of action. And like when I asked to have a CT scan midway through my chemotherapy treatment to see if the tumor was responding. Even though they don't typically do a scan at that point in the treatment, my knowledge about it helped me advocate for myself. I got the scan, and the results showed that the treatment was working. That gave me the confidence to keep going.

When it's time to make decisions, discuss the options with loved ones, a trusted friend, and members of your Executive Board. Not every decision will need input from everyone, but it's always a good idea to get second and third opinions, especially if you don't feel comfortable with the direction your doctor is going. If you feel uneasy or simply don't connect with them, get another opinion. Just because a decision is made doesn't mean it can't be changed or altered. Therapies are changed all the time.

When I was weighing my double mastectomy decision, I didn't flip a coin. I considered input from people who had been through breast cancer, I asked questions, and I debated with doctors. At the end of the day, the decision was mine, but I didn't make it alone.

Remember, you're the CEO of your health, and you sign off on the treatment, but a smart leader gathers data and considers input before they decide.

Step 5: Write Down Questions and Fears

When you're exhausted, nauseous, and foggy from treatment, you will forget things. That's why you write it all down. I kept a running list of questions. I even had a notepad next to my bed because I'd think of questions as I was falling asleep. Or I'd wake up at night with unsubstantiated fears running through my brain and needing a place to vent.

Write all your questions down, even if you think they're silly. No censorship is necessary because no questions are dumb. No fear is dumb. If you think your question is stupid, write it down and ask it anyway because you need to be informed.

If you've recently received your diagnosis, life probably seems surreal right now. You're still wrapping your head around what's happening. But you need to get into the mindset that your "journey," or whatever you want to call it, has begun. Cancer has arrived, like an uninvited guest, so it's better to get the answers you need to feel informed and empowered.

The benefit of having your questions written down is twofold. First, the doctors take you seriously because they see that you're prepared to have a conversation with them. Second, questions keep you focused. When your questions and fears live on paper, they stop disco dancing in your head at 3:00 a.m. They become action items to be addressed instead of that one-hit wonder playing on repeat.

Sometimes my agenda was filled with so many questions that I was worried we wouldn't have time to discuss them all. I wanted to know everything. In fact, I was five steps ahead. But the doctors didn't mind. They assured me that all of my questions would be answered, and they helped me prioritize what I needed to know first.

Something you don't realize is the emotional toll fear can have on you. I was so deep in consultant mode that I didn't realize I needed help emotionally. I was in operation mode, so busy ticking off boxes that I didn't notice how the undercurrent of stress was affecting me negatively.

I was used to being the one in charge, the one who took care of everything, so when I realized I needed help emotionally, it took the wind out of me. It took raw honesty to admit that constantly repeating the words *I'm okay, I'm okay, I'm okay* in my head was a sign I needed help.

As time went by, I realized that I was crying in the shower more often. I was mentally unable to get out of bed more often, and I experienced sadness frequently. Cancer was taking its toll on me. Granted, I was living in the middle of a shitstorm because of my parents' health issues, and my home being invaded by three goons who tried to steal our cars, but that was all the more reason to get help.

Fear and emotional decline are part of the process. When you write your thoughts down, they lose some of their power. So list out all your questions, journal about your fears, and get help when you need it.

Step 6: Start a Healing Playbook

This is where it all comes together. This step is the heart of the Healing Rebel Protocol. Your Healing Playbook is your portable command center. It's the binder where you track everything. Every piece of this journey is documented. Appointments, test results, scan reports, questions, treatment plans, medication, nutrition, and contact numbers all live here.

Your Healing Playbook might be a notebook, a spreadsheet, or an app. The format doesn't matter. What matters is that it exists and that you use it. With your Playbook, you become the CEO of your treatment:

- You track your daily progress like KPIs.
- You keep your Board informed and prevent miscommunication.
- You engage doctors in solution-oriented discussions.
- Your comeback becomes a strategic win instead of guesswork.

I used a binder, divided into sections, and I carried it to every single meeting and every single treatment. When the brain fog rolled in and my body was exhausted, my Healing Playbook was my anchor. It gave me back my sense of control in a season where everything was hazy. If I needed to, I could hand the binder off to my Executive Assistant, and they would have no problem finding the relevant information.

You can decorate your Playbook if you want. Color-code it with pens and highlighters, plaster it with Lisa Frank stickers, whatever sparks even the tiniest bit of joy. In fact, if you still have your high school Trapper Keeper, dust it off, and let it shine again.

Why the Healing Rebel Protocol Works

The Healing Rebel Protocol restores your confidence so that you can command your comeback. Instead of passively accepting treatment options, you actively manage them. I took control of my cancer. I took control of my healing. If that made me a rebel, I happily accepted the title.

The Healing Rebel Protocol can give you control too. It provides structure amid the chaos. It helps you lead your comeback with Power Moves that keep you moving forward, getting answers, and making informed decisions. Cancer is unpredictable, but your approach with this protocol is straightforward. With these six steps, you shift from being an overwhelmed, deer-in-the-headlights patient to a Healing Rebel with a strategy.

Your Next Move

Now that you know the six steps of the Healing Rebel Protocol, the question is: How do you apply it in your life?

That's where we'll go next. In the following chapter, we'll focus on the three key fundamental components you need to fully implement the Healing Rebel Protocol.

CHAPTER 8

The Three Foundations From Which to Build Your Comeback

The elevator doors opened, and I stepped in. My heart was thrumming, and my hands were shaking. Hurt and anger surged through me. Before the doors had a chance to close, I slid to the floor, sobbing. I was crushed. This was it. I had reached my breaking point.

Just moments before, in a room down the hall, I begged my mom to take the next life-saving step in her treatment. She had come out of a successful surgery, where the doctor removed a cancerous brain tumor that threatened to take her life. The radiologist stood at the end of her bed, explaining that the next step in the treatment was radiation. Radiation therapy would destroy any remaining cancer cells and significantly reduce the risk of recurrence. It could elongate her life. But she was emphatic: no radiation.

I tried to convince her to do the radiation, encouraging her, telling her we could fight this together. I had flown in from

Toronto to see her, having just completed a round of chemo the day before.

She looked at me, then at the radiologist, "No, I'm not doing it."

My mom had been through a lot leading up to this moment. She had buried her daughter, my sister, after she succumbed to cancer. My dad's health was deteriorating, and she was under a lot of stress caring for him as his Alzheimer's symptoms became more and more unmanageable.

And then, she had a stroke.

Because my dad's capacity was severely diminished, he was unable to call for emergency help, and my mom did not receive immediate treatment. When the doctor performed a scan to assess the damage from the stroke, something new was uncovered—a brain tumor. Without surgery, it would have taken her life within a month. Now, having been through a very successful brain surgery, it seemed she had given up.

I begged, "Please, Mom, I'm fighting because I don't want to die. I need you to fight with me. Let's fight together."

I was dumbfounded. I was in the middle of fighting for my life, and my mother was giving up on hers. This was madness! How dare she?

But she adamantly refused, saying that she didn't want radiation and wanted to go be with my sister…in heaven.

I ripped off my wig and waved it in front of her. By this point, I had lost my hair. I was as bald as an eagle.

I yelled, "Look at me! Look at me! I'm doing this. Let's do this together. Are you telling me I shouldn't fight?"

She looked tired and hauntingly calm when she answered, "If I were you, I would just give up and go be with your sister. Just let it go. I just want to die."

Utterly defeated, I walked out of the room. I called my brother and told him that I couldn't do this anymore. I didn't have the emotional strength to see her again, to be around someone who had given up on herself, on us.

That day, sobbing in the elevator as it went up and down, people getting on and off, tentatively asking if I was okay, was one of my lowest points.

Eventually, I found the strength to get up off the floor, and I went to see my dad. He didn't know my name anymore, but just being with him, hearing him sing Frank Sinatra songs, grounded me. It gave me the strength to get back on a plane and go home.

That conversation with my mom was our last. I went to see her again to say goodbye, even though I was still angry. But she was in a lot of pain and virtually unconscious due to a high dose of medication to keep her comfortable.

Within two weeks, she had passed on. Instead of celebrating my last chemo treatment, I was eulogizing her at her funeral.

You may not have faced the same struggles that I did, but you don't live in a bubble either. Life goes on regardless of your diagnosis. It continues to throw curveballs while you're busy fighting for your comeback.

Those last two weeks with my mom taught me what no doctor, test, or treatment could: Without having a positive outlook, trusting your intuition, and building mental resilience, you won't survive the battle.

For the Healing Rebel Protocol to work, you need a good foundation. So, let's talk about these key fundamentals.

Foundation #1: Stay Positive and Grounded

When you hear the words "you have cancer," it's natural for your mind to race immediately to the worst-case scenario. For me, fear, anger, and shock all came rushing in. And it's okay. You're allowed to feel the full range of emotions. It's a natural human response. But getting stuck in those emotions won't change the diagnosis. It won't help you move forward. Crying in the shower and screaming into your pillow might give you a short-lived release, but at the end of the day, you still have to face your prognosis.

Now here's the good news: There is something you can do to move forward. Something you have complete control over that can change your experience, and in many cases, your outcome. It's choosing to cultivate a positive outlook and stay grounded.

Choosing Positivity Without Denial

I don't recommend choosing positivity lightly. Staying positive doesn't mean pasting on a smile and pretending everything is fine when it's not. It also doesn't mean ignoring the challenges coming your way. You will have to deal with them. Staying positive means that even in the face of this dire situation, you take a step back and ask yourself critical questions like:

- What matters most to me right now?
- What's possible for me given my diagnosis, age, and circumstances?
- Am I looking for a cure, a remission, or to prolong my time on earth?

These questions help you cut through the noise and provide a benchmark from which to measure each decision you make. They ground you in reality instead of spiraling in fear.

For example, I knew that if I had received the same diagnosis at age 84, I might have chosen a different path. I likely wouldn't have pursued chemo because, for me, the tradeoff wouldn't have been worth it. I'm not being morbid or pessimistic; it's really just having clarity. Clarity is the ground on which positivity can actually stand.

Allowing Science to Ground You

Science also gave me a reason to hope. My diagnosis would have been a death sentence 25 years ago. Today, thanks to advances in cancer research, people are living with Stage IV cancers in ways we couldn't have imagined. The medical field is constantly innovating, which is one reason I'm so big on doing research. With many cancers, not just breast cancer, doctors' goals are no longer just about extending life by a few months. They are helping patients live long, meaningful lives. Doctors are your allies. They want you to live just as much as you want to.

Here's where emotional grounding comes in. Being positive is great, but without grounding, it can drift into denial, and denial makes you reckless. You need both. Being emotionally grounded means you acknowledge the fear without letting it run the show. It means you allow yourself to feel all the emotions—cry, rage, question "why me?" And then you come back to center. You get curious about your options, move forward with logic, and ground yourself in the steady belief that you are not powerless against your diagnosis.

Yes, cancer is unpredictable. You may not be able to control the ultimate outcome, but you can control your perspective as you command your comeback. You can choose to meet each new day with gratitude for the time you have. You can choose to lean into the science and the support you've built around you instead of throwing your hands up in despair. You can choose to ground yourself emotionally so you're clear-headed when it comes time to make the decisions that matter.

Positivity isn't a promise that everything will be okay. It's a foundation that, when paired with emotional grounding, becomes one of the most powerful assets in your comeback portfolio.

Fundamental Keys for Your Comeback

1. Build a positive foundation so that you can work from clarity, not fear.
2. Do your research and look to science and innovation for inspiration and answers.
3. Ground your emotions. Feel them and then release them before making decisions.

Foundation #2: Trust Your Intuition

When you're dealing with a complex and overwhelming diagnosis, it's tempting to go along with whatever protocol the doctors advise. After all, they're the experts, right? But here's the thing: No one knows your body, your history, and your tolerance better than you do. So what do you do? You trust your intuition.

Intuition is a gift, although it doesn't mean you rely solely on your gut feeling while rejecting medical advice. Trusting your intuition means making decisions that reflect your instincts while taking into consideration your research and the insights from your trusted medical professionals. It's making sure the decisions you make are what's right for you.

Doctors will put together the best plan they can. But it's based on protocols that might not be a good fit for you. That's why doing your research ahead of time is critical, and why it's one of the four Power Moves I shared in chapter 4. When you walk into the office with information and clarity, you're able to ask the right questions and push back if something doesn't feel right.

What Does Trusting Your Intuition Mean?

For me, trusting my intuition became very real when my doctor suggested a lumpectomy. On paper, it was the "right protocol." It was "good enough" to remove the cancerous mass, and it is standard procedure to save the breast. But because of my research and my high-risk status, I knew the recurrence rate was about 30%—too high for me to accept. It was a high enough statistic for me to say, "Take them both off." It wasn't an easy choice, but based on my research, my intuition told me this was the decision I could live with.

Trusting your intuition also means having a strategy before you're in the thick of it. For instance, when I wanted to try the cold cap to preserve my hair during chemo, I pushed for it, even though it meant adjusting to a different chemotherapy regimen. Ultimately, the cold cap didn't work, and I ended up losing my hair anyway, but that didn't matter. What mattered was that I honored my instincts and advocated for myself.

How to Balance Advice With Inner Knowing

Everyone around you will have an opinion on how you should treat your diagnosis. Your spouse, your friends, your family, and probably even a neighbor or two will have something to say. Some will support you wholeheartedly, while others will question your choices and try to convince you to take a different path. Their opinions may come from love, fear, or even their own need for comfort to know that you'll be okay. But the bottom line is: They don't have to live with the outcome. You do.

That's where trusting your intuition comes in. You can listen to well-meaning advice, but the decision is ultimately yours. When you make it from a place of inner knowing, you're far less likely to regret it later.

Trusting yourself sometimes means you take the harder path. I know I did. A double mastectomy is a much more difficult path than a lumpectomy. But giving away that power would have left me disconnected from my own healing journey. Even if the decisions were hard to make at times, I felt peace knowing that I trusted myself enough to make them.

Trusting your intuition is about ownership. It's aligning your doctor's medical advice with your own research and your intuition, and forming a plan that you can stand behind, even when it's tough.

Fundamental Keys for Your Comeback

1. Do your homework. You can't make aligned decisions without understanding what's at stake.

2. Trust your intuition. If something feels off, speak up and push for alternatives.

3. Own the outcome. Others can advise, but only you live with the results, so make the choices that give you peace.

Foundation #3: Build Mental Resilience

Life is already filled with ups and downs. Add in a diagnosis like cancer, and suddenly your roller coaster ride gets a few unexpected twists and turns. If you thought dealing with challenges was hard before, now you have to face the ugly truth head-on, decide how you'll respond, and find a way to keep moving forward.

That's where mental resilience comes in.

If you're going to make it to the end of this ride, you've got to be tough. Mental resilience doesn't mean white-knuckling your way through treatment and pretending you're strong every moment of every day. You're allowed to break down when you need to. Mental resilience equips you with the courage and stamina to wipe away the tears, put on your favorite lipstick, and dance your way into your next chemo treatment. How do you build mental resilience?

Choosing Self-Care and Support

The internet will give you plenty of mental resilience options, like learning coping mechanisms and practicing mindfulness. For me, it was really about two things: maintaining a healthy self-care regimen and getting professional support before the bottom fell out.

I've always been disciplined about health and fitness, even when I was flying in and out of multiple meetings every week. So I continued to exercise and make healthy meals as much as I could. The truth is, I had been given a death sentence, but I wasn't going down without a fight. I walked, hiked, boxed, weight trained, and played tennis. I also made sure I had plenty of downtime to rest and recover. This routine gave me a sense of normalcy during the chaos, which gave me mental resilience. I had a reason to get up and keep going every day.

Recognizing Your Breaking Point

If you've ever gone through something like this, you know there comes a time when you hit bottom. The moment I realized I truly needed help was during a time when I was dealing with a tsunami of events. My mom battled brain cancer, my dad struggled with Alzheimer's, and we experienced a home invasion. I was in the midst of my chemo treatments, and it was all too much. My mental resilience was cracking everywhere, fracturing the last bit of sanity I had left.

During one meeting, I'll never forget my surgeon asking, "Do you have help?" I assured her that my husband and friends supported me. She said, "No. Are *you* getting any help?"

I think she realized that I was hitting bottom, and her question hit home. It was a really scary realization for me because I always felt I was very grounded. I was always able to handle things on my own. I ran companies. I hired and fired people. I ran around the country and did a hundred things at once and came out on top. I mean, my chemo treatments were dance parties! To me, admitting that I needed help meant that this cancer thing was defeating me.

But she was right. I needed help. So I engaged with a psychiatrist and a psychologist, even though it was hard for me to accept. I even agreed to medication, something I'd always resisted. But I wasn't the same woman I used to be. Cancer had changed me, and pretending to be tough when I was falling apart only made things harder.

Mental resilience is a personal thing. For me, it meant tons of self-care and admitting that I wasn't invincible. That day, I added two new professionals to my Board of Advisers: a psychologist and a psychiatrist.

Now it's your turn. How will you build mental resilience?

Fundamental Keys for Your Comeback

1. Decide on what self-care habits you'll implement. Pick one and start today.

2. Notice when your resilience is cracking. Take action before you collapse.

3. Accept that your cancer or illness changes you. Building mental resilience helps you adapt.

Your Permission Slip to Command Your Comeback

The day I fell apart in the elevator was an excruciating wake-up call. My mom had given up, and there was nothing I could do to change her mind. She made her choice.

That wasn't going to be me. You see, I had also made a choice. I didn't want to die, and I was going to do everything in my power to come back from the devastation cancer had wreaked on my body and my life.

When cancer (or any major life crisis) barges into your world, it feels like everything you knew about yourself changes—as if you walked through a sliding door into an alternate reality. You don't get to choose what life throws at you, but you do get to choose the foundation from which you'll fight.

That's why these three fundamentals—staying positive and grounded, trusting your intuition, and building mental resilience—are so critical. They become the solid ground beneath your feet when everything tilts sideways.

A positive outlook, paired with emotional grounding, gives you clarity to see beyond the fear and uncertainty. It helps you move forward with intention, knowing that while you can't control everything, at least you can control your perspective.

Trusting your intuition keeps you aligned with yourself. It ensures the decisions you make reflect not only the medical advice but also your research, your values, and your inner compass. At the end of the day, you're the one who has to live with the outcome.

Mental resilience equips you for the long haul. It props you up and helps you weather the roller coaster of unexpected twists and turns.

Together, these three foundations make it possible for you to see the light at the end of the tunnel. You will not be the same person who walked into the doctor's office when you received your diagnosis. You will change. But with these foundations, you'll find the strength to adapt, the courage to speak up, and clarity to command your comeback on your terms. This isn't just about surviving; it's about refusing to surrender to something that thinks it has already won.

Now that you've learned the Healing Rebel Protocol and built a foundation from which to command your comeback, it's time to *become* a healing rebel.

In part three, I'll share a few key tips for finishing strong. You'll learn how to create a Cancer Response Plan, how to implement exercise and nutrition for optimal health as your body recovers, and why rest is essential. If you're ready, turn the page and let's begin.

PART 3

I'm Not Just a Cancer Survivor. I'm a Healing Rebel.

CHAPTER 9

Create a Cancer Response Plan

When cancer bullies its way into your life, it feels like chaos has set up camp in your living room. One day, you're running your business, taking care of your family, and juggling life's ups and downs. Next, you're walking out of the doctor's office feeling the earth shift underfoot. The diagnosis changes everything. It's paralyzing and can make you feel like you've lost all sense of control.

But I'm here to reassure you that control is never completely gone. Sure, cancer has invaded your body, but it's still *your* body. You get to take charge of how you respond.

In my business career, I walked into many failing companies, along with some that were successful and wanted to become more productive. Each one carried its own type of "sickness"— something hidden or overlooked that was causing it to crash. My job as a consultant was to diagnose the problem, treat it, and create a plan for ongoing success. That often meant creating a crisis response plan that would guide the company out of crisis and chart a sustainable path forward.

When I was diagnosed with cancer, I instinctively drew on those same skills. I treated my diagnosis like I would a company in crisis: I methodically gathered facts, identified the root issues, and developed a response plan. Just as I had done in boardrooms and strategy sessions, I created a roadmap to navigate through my cancer crisis with the intention of building a foundation for long-term success. I call it my Cancer Response Plan.

A Cancer Response Plan brings order to the chaos and calm to the mind. It doesn't make the diagnosis go away, but it gives you a roadmap to follow, putting the power back in your hands. The steps in the Healing Rebel Protocol laid out in chapter 7 start you down the path to navigating treatment. The Cancer Response Plan is an extra layer of defense, making it easier for you to work through the six steps.

Creating Your Cancer Response Plan

When companies face a crisis, a good leader doesn't just cross their fingers and hope a solution presents itself. A good leader gets to work. They gather information, define priorities, and set clear action steps. It's a leadership mindset, and it's the same mindset you'll adopt here. You need to think like a crisis manager and take charge—because you are the CEO of your comeback.

Ask yourself:

- What decisions need to be made now?

- Who can I rely on for help?
- How will I share information about my wishes and my treatment?
- Who needs to be informed, and at what level? Think family, colleagues, and clients.
- Will I continue to work or take time off?

Asking yourself questions like these can help you build your Cancer Response Plan. To make it easier for you, I've put together four areas that you should consider including in your plan:

1. Delegate and automate responsibilities.
2. Organize your paperwork.
3. Choose a communication tool.
4. Make work accommodations.

Let's take a closer look at each of these, beginning with how to delegate and automate responsibilities.

Delegate and Automate Responsibilities

One of the fastest lessons I learned when cancer tried to take over my body was that my energy was an essential commodity. I had to guard it carefully. Cancer treatments drain you in ways you might not anticipate. It wasn't just physical exhaustion, but also mental and emotional exhaustion. You can't spend your precious energy completing every household task and worrying about what to cook for dinner.

Delegation and automation are the answers. The person you were before—wife, mom, boss—is currently out of the office.

Your primary responsibility now is to take care of yourself first. Delegation and automation are survival strategies.

Here's what you do:

Select a point person. Think of them as your Executive Assistant. They track appointments, manage calls, and filter information. If you completed step 2 in the Healing Rebel Protocol, you already have this person lined up.

Automate what you can. Grocery delivery, childcare help, house cleaning, recurring bill payments, and anything else you can think of.

Decide what happens with work responsibilities. Whether you work for yourself or someone else, you'll need to take a step back. Even if you want to keep working through your treatment, you may not be able to. Prepare to push pause or scale back operations.

I fought against taking leave from my work. My instinct as a leader was to keep going, to push through. It's all I've ever known. But, after a few honest conversations with my team, I agreed to step away and take the time off to focus on my health, especially after the profound personal losses I experienced alongside my cancer treatments.

As a consultant, I've often told companies that sometimes you need to pause, address the underlying issues, and create a crisis plan before moving forward. Now, I had to apply that principle to myself. At the time, I felt it was a weakness that I couldn't do it all. But looking back, I now see it as an act of strength. Pushing pause and stepping back gave me the space to heal, reset, and rebuild—not just physically, but also with renewed purpose, resilience, and clarity for my future. Taking time off gave me the bandwidth and the energy to focus on survival. That's why step 1 of the Healing Rebel Protocol is Pause Before You Panic.

Organize Your Paperwork

Just as companies keep legal documents to protect themselves, you need to organize your personal affairs. We've talked about this before in step 3 of the Healing Rebel Protocol, and I'm revisiting it again here, plus a few extra items, because it's so important. Getting your legal affairs in order might feel a little morbid, but it's the most loving and kind thing you can do for your family. A binder or digital file, shared with your attorney or a trusted family member, can save enormous stress later. Consider including at least three sections in your binder or digital file. You'll need a legal and financial section that includes the following:

- Power of attorney
- Will and trust documents
- Executor information
- Living will or advance directives
- Guardianship designations
- Beneficiary designations for retirement accounts, pensions, and insurance policies

Include a section for your household and business-related information:

- Tax records (personal and business) plus instructions on who should handle final filings
- Property deeds and vehicle titles
- Password and account access (bank, credit card, mortgage, utilities, subscriptions)

Don't forget to make space for personal and relational items:

- Letters to loved ones
- Personal journals and personal history information
- Social media account instructions for memorialization or closure
- Funeral arrangements and burial wishes
- Organ donation registration (if applicable)

You can create a separate legal binder with all of this information inside. Or create a digital file on your computer. Make sure your attorney and a trusted family member have access.

I saw firsthand what happens when legal documents and designations aren't in place when my father fell ill. My parents didn't have a power of attorney established. Their money was frozen, and we couldn't access funds to care for him. Thankfully, my brother and I had resources to step in, but the stress could have been avoided. Getting my paperwork in order gave me peace of mind, knowing that it provided clarity if anything should happen to me.

Getting your paperwork in order is another way for you to control your narrative when the rest of your life feels out of balance. You decide how your wishes are carried out. And that is part of being a Healing Rebel.

Choose a Communication Tool

During your treatment, people will want updates. Family and close friends may want to text you to see how you're doing. At some point, though, answering questions and sending the same information to 20 different people becomes exhausting.

Text groups can be overwhelming for you and everyone in the group. Sharing on social media is an option, but not everyone has social media, and you may not want to share your personal experiences on those types of platforms. Instead, look for a group chat app (see examples in this book's appendix) to exchange messages.

Whatever communication tool you choose, it will become invaluable, especially as you build your inner circle. Take another look at Power Move #4 in chapter 4 for more about building your inner circle.

One tool that helped me was a no-cost nonprofit health platform where I could easily post updates, share important information, and ask for help. It was a private communication hub that gave me control over what information I shared and with whom, while saving my energy and my sanity. Think of it as your corporate communication channel. It's a way to update the "stakeholders" without draining the CEO.

Make Work Accommodations

For me, stepping away from work was painful. I loved my job. I thrived in it, and I didn't know how to *not* work. In a way, I felt like I was abandoning my team, but also my persona, my identity. I was Farla Efros, President and CEO. Who did cancer think it was trying to take that away from me?

But the truth was that I couldn't continue to operate at the same level while going through treatment. It wasn't fair to my team or to my clients.

When I went on leave, I thought I could cheat the system a little. Cancer had already stripped so much away, and I wasn't ready to give up work too. So I stayed tethered to a major client, quietly answering emails, reviewing plans, and convincing myself that I could balance both worlds.

But HR noticed. After several conversations, they sat me down and said plainly: If I was going to be on leave, then I had to actually be on leave. No more half in, half out.

I cried that day. Not just a misty eyed tear or two, but the kind of racking sobs that come from deep in your chest; the kind that steals your breath because it felt like I was losing yet another part of myself. Cancer had already stolen my energy, my hair, my sense of safety, my body as I once knew it—and now it wanted my work too. My identity. The part of me that was measured in deliverables, deadlines, and strategy decks.

It wasn't about the client or the project; It was about me. Who was I if I wasn't fixing problems, steering teams, and building crisis plans? For years, that's how I defined myself. Work was where I was strong, where I knew the rules and could win. Without it, I felt untethered—like someone had pulled the floor out from under me.

That day, I realized the hardest part of stepping back wasn't the silence of an empty inbox or the fear of being forgotten. It was learning to exist without the armor of productivity and to accept that pausing wasn't failure; it was survival.

Inevitably, you'll have to decide for yourself whether or not you can continue to work and in what capacity. Depending on your illness and treatment, you might be able to work part-time. You'll need to have an honest conversation with your Human Resources department or direct manager to see what accommodations or options are available. If you own your business, it may mean empowering your team to step up or temporarily pausing projects so you don't overextend yourself.

The bottom line is that you need to have boundaries in place. If you can't afford to take extended time off, block off sections of time each day and week for treatments and rest. Decline unnecessary meetings and whittle down your responsibilities to the bare minimum. Delegate the rest. The goal is to preserve the energy you need for healing.

A Cancer Response Plan Provides Peace of Mind

When I was first diagnosed, I didn't hesitate. I jumped into action and began making plans. That's the leader in me, and I'm glad I did. My treatment protocol consumed more energy than I imagined. Brain fog crept in, and even simple tasks felt monumental. That's why it's crucial to build a plan.

At the heart of a Cancer Response Plan is the reminder that you are still in control. By delegating responsibilities, getting your paperwork in order, and choosing a communication tool, you give yourself the gift of control and also peace of mind.

You can't command cancer cells to vacate the premises or tell your hair to stay put, but you can control how you prepare. Having a plan makes it easier to act instead of react. Just knowing you have a plan in place sends a powerful signal to yourself and to those around you that you are not just a patient; you are a Healing Rebel.

Healing Rebel Reflections

Now it's your turn. Grab a journal and write down your first steps:

- What decisions do I need to make now?
- Who can I delegate to?
- What paperwork or documents do I need to organize?
- How will I handle work responsibilities?

Remember, a Cancer Response Plan isn't about controlling every outcome. It's about reclaiming enough control to ease your mind so that you can preserve your energy for healing.

One of the main keys to healing is providing your body with the nutrients it needs to battle illness. And that's where we're going next. Chapter 10 is all about strengthening your body and mind through nutrition and exercise.

Strengthen Your Body Through Nutrition and Exercise

I had always been healthy. Not in an overzealous health nut way, but I was purposeful and intentional about nutrition and exercise. I ate healthy, well-balanced meals and was very active. So when cancer came calling, I felt like my body had betrayed me.

Of course, I had snacks and indulged in dessert occasionally, but I just felt better when I ate well. Food was not only fuel for my workouts but fuel for my job. My mind had to be sharp and laser-focused, and good nutrition provided the nutrients I needed to think clearly.

Fast forward to chemotherapy, and I started losing weight. At one point, I had lost 30 pounds and didn't recognize the woman looking back at me from the mirror. I wanted to eat, but it was hard to consume enough food when I felt so nauseated all the time. Everything tasted like metal, and I had mouth sores that were next level. They hurt so badly that I just couldn't bear to eat food of any kind. At one meeting, after noticing my weight loss, the doctor told me to eat whatever I could tolerate, "even if it's fast food."

I looked at her like she had lost her mind. With everything I was fighting through, the last thing I wanted to do was feed my body processed food that might fuel cancer growth. I understood her point—that calories were better than no calories—but I just couldn't bring myself to eat food that wasn't good for my body. Plus, any extra salt in the foods I ate made my mouth sores even worse.

At that point, I didn't recognize my own body or mind. My energy level had tanked, and it was as if someone had installed a fog machine in my brain. But I still kept forcing myself to put one foot in front of the other, and one thing I knew for sure was that putting fast food into my body wasn't going to help when it was struggling to fight this cancerous invasion.

Good nutrition became a form of rebellion. I wasn't going to use cancer as an excuse to eat junk food. Instead, I became extremely intentional about what I put into my body. But my basic healthy-girl protocol wasn't good enough anymore. I needed to take it up a notch. I took what I was already doing—eating well-rounded, nutritious meals—and bumped it up to the next level. It was a way of fighting back that was completely within my power.

I'm not a doctor or nutritionist. I'm definitely not a wellness influencer. I'm just a woman who wasn't going to give up when my body turned on me. No matter what, I was going to fight.

But in order to fight, I had to give my body what it needed to heal.

Nutrition Protocol: Fuel to Fight

Every good plan needs an end goal, and mine was threefold: reduce inflammation, increase my energy, and get my cognitive function back, at least as much as I could.

I did my homework, combing through scientific and naturopathic health journals and bookmarking cancer websites. I studied cancer-fighting diets and the power of superfoods. On some level, perhaps I was hoping to find the magic bean, a secret antidote hidden away in a dense tropical location, the one thing that would make me well again. (Hint: It doesn't exist.)

I read everything I could find on inflammation, antioxidants, and herbs for cognitive recovery. I studied detoxification methods and how to help and support my body's natural detoxification processes. Chemotherapy might pump me full of toxins, but I wasn't going to invite them to set up camp once they did their job.

I researched the benefits of juicing and the advantages of celery juice, tart cherry juice, wild blueberry juice, and spinach. Cruciferous vegetables and kiwi fruit also made the cut. I tried them all. And with each celery juice shot, I raised my glass and declared, "F you, cancer!"

I want to take a moment here to say that the protocols and regimens I tried are what felt good for me. I'm going to share them with you in this chapter, but please keep in mind that I'm not a doctor, nutritionist, or exercise therapist. I'm not passing out prescriptions or remedies.

Through trial and error, I cobbled together a routine that worked for my unique body and circumstances. Your situation and body are unique to you, and that's why I'm not going to give you a detailed plan to copy. I'll share what I learned, and then it's up to you to take it and create your very own nutrition and exercise plan.

The truth is, I don't know if everything I tried worked on a cellular level. Maybe it was all just a placebo effect. If so, that's okay with me. All I know is that I felt better when I ate well and exercised, and that's what got me through the worst fight of my life. My hope is that my simple protocol will help you too.

My Morning Routine Is a Full-Time Job

Throughout my treatment, I stuck to a regimented routine, never missing a step. Today, I continue with most, if not all, of these steps every morning because my post-treatment body still needs a lot of encouragement. Who knew getting out of bed and starting my day would be so dramatic, not only during treatment, but also afterward?

One of the most effective hacks I found to facilitate a healthy body and mind was humor. Cancer wrecked my life, but when I could laugh about it, the hours and days felt better.

Whether you're going through treatment right now or find yourself on the other side, like me, I hope you'll see the humor in the madness.

So, with that, I give you My Morning Routine.

Step 1: Unlocking the Body (AKA Human Origami)

Waking up is less "rise and shine" and more "click, pop, creak." My knees lock, my feet freeze, and my hands do their best mannequin impression. It takes a solid hour of stretching, grimacing, and negotiating with my joints just to walk like a semi-evolved human. At this point, I don't hop out of bed—I rise from it like the Bride of Frankenstein.

The truth is, joint pain is no laughing matter. It's depressing and debilitating, plus, it slows me down. To help unlock my joints, I use the MEAT protocol. It's an alternative to the RICE (Rest, Ice, Compression, Elevation) protocol for managing musculoskeletal injuries, but I use it to promote healing in my joints and reduce stiffness. The MEAT protocol stands for: Movement, Exercise, Analgesia, Treatment.

I start with gentle movement to work out the kinks to help with mobility and range of motion. It's like a warm-up session. Next, I participate in a variety of exercises from strength training to cardio. The key with exercise is to listen to your body. Push yourself gently, but don't overdo it. After exercise, I'll use a pain reliever (analgesic) if needed to manage discomfort. But again, use caution when taking pain relievers. Lastly, the T stands for treatment, which can include massage or chiropractic treatments.

Step 2: The Hipster Cappuccino of Life

After an hour of getting my body to move and bend again, it's reward time. I carefully craft the most divine cappuccino— with oat milk, because dairy and I broke up in 2018. With chemotherapy treatments, I got enough chemicals for a lifetime delivered right into my veins, so I use an app when shopping to scan my food to check whether it's clean or chemical soup. My oat milk scored 98/100, so obviously I framed the results.

You can use an app, like I did, to scan the barcode or ingredient list. The app analyzes your food and lets you know if it contains anything you'd rather steer clear of. Some apps even allow you to flag ingredients you want to avoid due to allergies or intolerances. The point is that knowing what's in your food helps you make better choices. When your body is healing, you've got to give it the best.

Step 3: Lemon Water With a Kick

Next, I chug lemon water like a wellness influencer mid-detox. But wait—plot twist. I add RestoraLax because chemotherapy and pain meds produce some not-so-fun side effects. Constipation, anyone? My stomach is basically a diva who refuses to perform without fiber and a contract. So, I do what I can to help things move along, starting with hydration. Lemon juice flavors my water and helps the RestoraLax go down easier, but it also provides vitamin C, a terrific antioxidant for immunity.

Step 4: Celery Juice—Because Why Be Happy?

Then I juice an entire forest of celery, AKA the bitter, crunchy regret stick. It tastes like grass and seawater had a baby, but it gives me energy and an irrational sense of superiority.

"But why celery juice?" you ask. "Why not literally anything else?"

Some say it's a placebo; its benefits are unproven. But I drink it for the antioxidants, flavonoids, and anti-inflammatory compounds. Remember, one of my main goals is to reduce inflammation, so placebo or not, it's my daily dare to the universe. I drink it like a shot of tequila and whisper, "For the mitochondria."

Step 5: The Juice Flight of Champions

Next, it's juice tasting time. I rotate between tart cherry, wild blueberry, and pomegranate because clearly I moonlight as a sommelier for antioxidant beverages.

Each one is diluted with water because pure pomegranate juice could melt enamel, and sometimes I toss in creatine and protein powder, just in case I spontaneously join CrossFit.

Once again, this juice rotation is all about antioxidants and anti-inflammatories. All three of these juices can help with muscle recovery and reduce soreness after exercise. Step 5 hits all three of my requirements: reduce inflammation, increase my energy, and get my cognitive function back.

If you haven't heard, creatine isn't just for gym bros building muscle. Creatine supplementation can improve cognitive function.

Step 6: Prune and Kiwi Party

To close the show, I eat five or six prunes and a couple of kiwis because even after everything I've consumed, my digestive system still needs a gentle threat. Kiwis provide fiber, vitamins, and a little energy kick. Prunes aren't just for grandma; they're the "closer" of this operation. They show up like, "Move over, amateurs. I've got this." It's me, my prunes, and a dream.

The Science and Sanity Behind the Circus

During my treatment, my meal prep was simple: proteins, vegetables, complex carbohydrates, and fruits. When I didn't feel well enough to eat food, I made a high-nutrient shake.

With nutrition, my goal was to support my body's healing and recovery in the following ways:

- Reduce inflammation
- Support digestion and detoxification
- Support healthy blood sugar levels
- Rebuild energy
- Repair gut microbiomes
- Restore cognition (that's the blue-sky dream)

I said before that if all of this nutrition was just a placebo effect, I'd be okay with that. And I am. But I believe that owning my nutrition did help my body fight cancer and heal.

For one thing, my bloodwork always came back perfect, even with all of the toxins in my body; none were showcased in my blood. So, something was working. I even had COVID while going through chemo and got through it with the help of extra vitamins, rest, and my mixtape playlist from 1985.

After chemotherapy, you have to repair your body. Your microbiomes (gut, skin, oral, respiratory, and reproductive) have been eviscerated, so you'll need to systematically rebuild the beneficial bacteria by consuming good prebiotic and probiotic foods.

Prebiotics are non-digestible carbohydrates that serve as food for the beneficial bacteria already living in your gut microbiome. Prebiotic foods include legumes, garlic, onions, asparagus, and more.

Probiotics are live microorganisms that improve gut and mental health, boost immunity, and assist nutrient absorption. These are very important little diva bugs. You'll find them in fermented foods like yogurt, sauerkraut, kimchi, and kombucha.

Chemotherapy can also weaken your immune system, making it harder to fight off sickness. Sugar and processed foods diminish your immune system even further, and that's why good nutrition is critical.

The key is to show up for your health every day. Put the good stuff in your body, and you'll see the evidence shine through in the health of your skin, hair, nails, organs, and bloodwork. You'll also feel better and recover faster. When I focused on my nutrition, I had peace of mind knowing that I was giving my body what it needed to fight.

That doesn't mean you can't have a glass of wine or indulge in dessert. It's all about balance. But the more you focus on good nutrition, the better you'll feel. Today, I still include wild blueberries, tart cherries, kiwi fruit, sweet potato, and celery juice in my routine. It just reassures me that if cancer were to attack my body again, I'd be ready to fight.

Hopefully, this has given you a glimpse into why nutrition is key to fighting cancer and recovering from treatment. But we're only halfway there. Exercise is the next thing you'll want to focus on. While I'm not going to give you a spreadsheet with a workout routine, I will share with you how exercise was my saving grace.

Exercise: My Saving Grace

Before I talk about exercise from the lens of a cancer patient, I want to point out that exercise was always important to me *before* I got cancer. I was already participating in different types of exercise, so my body was conditioned to continue working out through my treatment. That may not be the case for you, and that's okay. Start where you are and do what you can. Even if all you can manage is a walk to the mailbox and back, it's a place to start and something to be proud of.

When I started my treatment, the doctors strongly suggested that I stop my workout routine. They said, "Save your energy. Rest as much as you can." That's not bad advice, really. You do need to rest to recover. But what they didn't know was that exercise *was* my energy.

If you've learned anything about me, you know I like to dance to the beat of my own '80s synth drum, and I wasn't about to stop doing the one thing that made me feel normal.

My Exercise Routine Kicks Ass

Movement wasn't something I did to tick a box; it was the thread that held me together. I had always been active before cancer, so why on earth would I stop just because chemo showed up? If anything, it became more important than ever. Every workout reminded me that I was still alive, I was powerful, and I could kick cancer's ass.

Kickboxing: The Release

Kickboxing became my rebellion. Every punch, every kick, was aimed at something bigger than the bag in front of me. Fear. Anger. Helplessness. I didn't look like myself anymore, but when I was sweating, I *felt* like myself. For those rounds, I wasn't "the woman with cancer." I was just me.

Tennis: The Rhythm

Tennis was another anchor. I wasn't worried about winning points. I was finding my rhythm, chasing the ball across the court, and remembering that my body could still respond. It could still surprise me. Some days I was fast, some days I was dragging, but every time I picked up that racket, it was proof: I'm still here. I'm still moving.

Weight Lifting: The Strength

Weight lifting gave me something even deeper: strength, both physical and emotional. Picking up those weights wasn't about vanity or sculpting muscle; it was my way of fighting back against the weakness chemo tried to tattoo into my bones. I thought about bone loss, about how fragile cancer treatment can make you, and every rep felt like reclaiming a little bit of that stolen territory. Lifting made me feel powerful. It gave me a sense of control when everything else was so wildly out of my hands.

Walking and Hiking: The Reset

Walking, well, walking saved me. On days when the nausea or fatigue pinned me down, I told myself, "just five minutes." I wasn't looking for a marathon. I was looking for a quick win, something to remind me I wasn't completely swallowed by chemo. The warm sun on my face, the breeze tickling my skin, the sound of my feet on the path; those tiny milestones became huge victories.

Here's the truth: Exercise wasn't about intensity. Not anymore. It was about humanity. Even the smallest movement made me feel like I had reclaimed a little piece of myself. If you've ever exercised before, you know what I mean. Exercise is power. It's life. When you're in the throes of chemotherapy, feeling drained and weak, you'll take any morsel of power you can get.

To me, power was important—I built a career on it. But now, I have to fight for power, especially when it comes to my brain.

Brain Power: A Word About Brain Fog

I used to think brain fog was just forgetting why you walked into a room. Cute, right?

Well, cancer brain fog is not cute. Instead of just losing your keys, you lose the part of your brain that remembered you even had keys. Cancer brain fog is your prefrontal cortex, hippocampus, and white matter all waving tiny white flags, wondering how you got here and desperate for help.

When it comes to the many flavors of brain fog, I've sampled them all:

- Short-circuit fog: The word is on the tip of your tongue… then vanishes into thin air.
- GPS fog: You know where you're going…until you don't. (Why did I come into the laundry room?)
- Hamster-wheel fog: Thoughts run and run but go nowhere. An endless ride.
- Static fog: Someone is talking, but all you hear is static. Their words don't compute.

I used to have a CEO brain. It was sharp and hyper-focused. I could multitask and make quick decisions without breaking my stride. My brain used to run boardrooms; now, it sputters and halts like dial-up internet. Yet, I still have to show up and speak. I still have to make good decisions because my life depends on it.

So, I do what I've always done—I fix it.

The Rewiring Begins

I know my brain is not broken; it's just bruised. It can respond to challenges if given the right care and feeding. Through trial and error, I've built a toolkit to navigate brain fog, rebuild synapses, and strengthen cognitive function in the hope that one day, I'll wake up with a clear mind, smile, and say, "I'm back!"

To Rewire the Prefrontal Cortex

When multi-tasking is a fantasy and making decisions feels as slow as molasses, try these tools:

1. Aerobic exercise: A ten-minute walk or dance party pumps blood and oxygen to closed circuits.

2. Mindfulness and meditation: Sit comfortably and spend five minutes focusing on your breathing. If your mind wanders, bring it back to your breath.

3. Nutrition: Add magnesium L-threonate to enhance memory, focus, and overall cognitive performance.

To Rewire the Hippocampus

When your short-term memory plays hide-and-seek with your keys, names, and conversations, try these tools:

1. Sleep: Your mind and body repairs itself during sleep. Guard it fiercely.

2. Learn new skills: Do puzzles, try a new dance step, or learn a new language to flex memory muscles.

3. Nutrition: Add DHA, a crucial omega-3 fatty acid for brain, eye, and nervous system development. You'll find it in fish, eggs, chia seeds, flaxseeds, and walnuts. Or you can try a quality fish or krill oil supplement.

To Rewire White Matter (Myelin)

When nerve signals creak to a halt, forming words is an Olympic sport, and your brain just feels tired of thinking, try these tools:

1. Resistance training: Whether you use body weight, resistance bands, or dumbbells, resistance training strengthens your body and promotes white matter health.

2. Learn new skills: Learn how to play an instrument or try a new experience. Anything to wake up your brain and give it something different to think about.

3. Nutrition: Eat foods high in B vitamins, vitamin D, and vitamin E (animal products, leafy greens, and legumes). Lion's mane mushroom is also considered good for nerve growth.

To Rewire the Amygdala and Fix Emotional Circuits

When estrogen deprivation has stress circuits on overdrive, and brain fog is giving you an anxiety meltdown, try these tools:

1. Yoga and tai chi: Calming movements and gentle stretching awaken the body while reining in the overactive amygdala.

2. Journaling: Get the noise out of your head and onto paper to remind yourself that you still have control.

3. Nutrition: Omega-3 rich foods or a daily supplement help calm neuroinflammation and stabilize your mood.

To Rewire the Wandering Mind

When your brain is stuck in fog mode and switching the track to focus mode is an uphill battle, try these tools:

1. Structured routines: Reduce decision fatigue by limiting the number of decisions you make each day.

2. Train the brain: Use brain training apps like Lumosity, Elevate, or CogniFit to sharpen your memory and attention.

3. Nutrition: Reduce your intake of extra sugar and carbs, and increase your intake of iron-rich foods with healthy fats to feed your brain.

The Truth About Your Brain

Even armed with all of these tools, the hardest battle is accepting that I might never be the CEO again. That woman—sharp, fearless, and commanding—is gone. And I mourn her every day.

Yet, I fight anyway. I focus on nutrition and exercise. I meditate, journal, play mind games (the good kind); I do the work of rewiring my brain. Through it all, I hold onto hope, because I'm stubborn that way, and I know that one day, I'll look in the mirror and recognize her again. Not the old CEO, not the woman before cancer, but a new version, slightly bruised, maybe a little off-kilter, but rewired, resilient, and still unapologetically me.

Start Where You Are

I'm not asking you to run a marathon. I'm just asking you to walk to the mailbox. And then walk to the end of the block. Stretch while you're waiting for the kettle to boil. Step outside and breathe. These little moments add up. Not in calories burned or muscles gained, but in the quiet rebellion of saying, "I'm still me. I'm still alive."

It's all too easy to let the couch become your best friend—your safe space. It will wrap its cozy arms around you and whisper, "Stay with me. I'll take care of you."

Don't listen to your couch, or your bed, or wherever you find yourself languishing. You have to train your brain to be strong just as much as you train your body—and it starts with getting up off the couch.

Because here's the thing: Exercise releases endorphins, and endorphins can help you feel better. So, channel your inner Elle Woods and make a case for getting up off the couch. If you need a little motivation, let me tell you what endorphins can do:

- Relieve pain
- Reduce stress, anxiety, and depression
- Enhance moods and boost self-esteem
- Support a healthy immune system
- Support cognitive function

Exercise clears your head and allows you to feel more like yourself, so find pockets in your day to move. Some days, you may only manage a little light stretching. Other days, you'll feel invincible. The point is to make exercise a priority because it might be the only thing that makes you feel normal again.

Exercise during chemo didn't cure the pain. It didn't stop the side effects. But it gave me something just as powerful: moments of normalcy. In the middle of cancer, those moments mattered more than anything. After losing so much to cancer, those precious minutes when I exercised reminded me that cancer didn't define me. I wasn't cancer. I was just me, Farla, in the gym, kicking butt, and taking names.

A Word of Caution

I didn't step up to the bag alone, and I didn't lift weights without a spotter. I had a trainer who understood my situation, who helped me with my form, knew when to push me, and when to take it slower. Sometimes I would go into the gym completely out of it with brain fog, not even sure what weight I needed. With my trainer's help, the fog began to clear, and after the workout, I left the gym feeling clear-headed and accomplished.

Now, I didn't go completely rogue and ignore my doctor's recommendations. In each meeting, I opened up my Healing Playbook (step 6 of the Healing Rebel Protocol) and reviewed my nutrition and exercise regimen with them. We talked about how I felt before and after treatments, what foods and exercises made me feel better, and how I could best prepare for the next treatment.

Please listen to your healthcare providers, and if you have the opportunity to work with a trainer, I highly recommend it. If you don't have a trainer, most hospitals have wellness programs to help patients with exercise and nutrition. Another option is to enlist a few friends to be your workout buddies. If you struggle putting together nutritious meals, use the resources offered at your hospital to get in touch with a nutritionist.

Reclaim the Body That Betrayed You

Even when I thought my body failed me, I refused to abandon it. When you're a healing rebel, that's just what you do. Nutrition plus exercise is a winning combination, and it kept me going on days when the couch kept calling. It gave me something to look forward to that wasn't another meeting.

Cancer wasn't my permission slip to be lazy; I've never taken the easy way out. For me, nutrition and exercise became daily nonnegotiables. Was I perfect at them? Not even close. But did I do my best to show up every single day? Absolutely.

I'm not a doctor, but I did survive cancer, drink celery juice voluntarily, and once made a spreadsheet for my antioxidant rotation. It may seem a little bit extra, but after chemo, surgery, hormone therapy, and enough scans to glow in the dark—I'll do whatever it takes to feel 5% better.

So here's to the routine, the potions, and the lovely prunes, and the sheer audacity of calling this "self-care" when it's clearly a full-blown phytochemical Broadway show. Now it's your turn to take the stage. Would you like an antioxidant with that?

CHAPTER 11

Rest, Recharge, and Live Fully

Exercise was my saving grace, and my nutrition protocol helped me feel like I could get through one more day—even one more round of chemo. But sometimes, it all became too much. That's when I gave myself permission to stop pushing so hard.

I remember one day in particular. I was so tired. I knew I needed to get up, get moving, and go to the gym. But my body wouldn't cooperate; it was too tired to move. So, I stayed in bed. When the guilt began to creep in, I swatted it away because rest is just as important for recovery as exercise and nutrition. The funny thing is that my day didn't fall apart because I didn't exercise. As soon as I decided to stay in bed and not feel bad about it, something magical happened. I felt…relief.

You don't always need to push yourself to the limit to prove you are strong. Resting doesn't mean you're giving up. It means you understand that your body and mind need time to rest because rest is where the rebuilding happens. It's all part of the process, and the truth is that rest can be just as productive as action.

So if you're reading this and you feel guilty for lying down in the middle of the day, don't. There is strength in resting. Even warriors need naps.

Redefining Rest as Strength

Even the best CEOs and business owners take time off. When I was running companies, I understood that I couldn't operate at peak performance on an empty tank. Pushing through, no matter what, can lead to mistakes. Instead of thinking that I had to keep up appearances and prove I was strong by not letting up, I always took time to rest and recharge, so I could come back even stronger.

Fighting cancer is no different. During treatment, rest isn't a reward for checking everything off your to-do list; it's a requirement for staying alive. Believe me, I know how hard it is to slow down, especially when you're used to moving at a hundred miles an hour; it's the curse of the achievement-oriented personality.

But it's important to listen to your body when it whispers instead of waiting for it to scream. Sometimes, it's okay to lose the argument with your brain when it's telling you to move and let your body win this round. It's a mindset shift, really. You have to redefine what strength is. Instead of looking at needing rest as a weakness, what if you decided that rest was a strength?

When I allowed myself to rest without guilt, I saw how much more energy and clarity I had. I actually felt stronger after resting. Some of the brain fog lifted, and I was able to refocus. Instead of wasting energy pretending to be okay, I used that energy to recover and *become* okay.

Sleeping in and taking naps isn't the only way to rest. You can also engage in active rest days. Active rest is a way to move your body and get a little exercise without taking a complete rest day. On the days when I didn't have enough energy to throw a right hook in boxing or volley a tennis ball across the net, I chose something easier, like walking, Pilates, or gentle stretching.

If you've spent your life at the head of the class, achieving, leading, and solving problems, rest will feel unnatural at first. You might feel lazy or unmotivated. But give yourself grace. Healing requires you to redefine success.

Recharge Through Living Fully

During one of my appointments, while waiting to be called back, I made a bucket list of all the places I wanted to go and adventures I wanted to have. Sitting in that waiting room, riffing ideas with my friend, I decided that I would reward myself with a trip after every chemo treatment.

I went hiking all over Utah, and I visited Palm Springs and lots of places in Florida. I went to Mexico and overseas to explore Spain. I traveled like crazy. It gave me something to look forward to, and it was beneficial to my mental health. Knowing that I was going to go on an adventure afterward helped me to deal with the nausea and life-sucking process that is chemotherapy.

There's a lot of controversy about traveling during treatment, but if you haven't guessed by now, I'm always going to do what I want. I've never been one who followed all the rules. Traveling was my way of being able to forget about cancer for a few days. It was a way to escape the cancer life and feel normal again.

Of course, I knew I still had cancer; I had the bald head to prove it! I felt terrible and couldn't eat much. But I found immense joy in getting away for a few days. For me, it was another piece of my healing protocol.

I went on these trips with my husband or friends, so I was never alone. And it was great! I did what I could physically manage and took it easy when I didn't feel well.

One trip in particular is quite memorable because I nearly died. Well, maybe not nearly, but I did end up in the ER.

Just after my last chemo treatment, Mik and I decided to meet up with our daughter in the south of France for a family getaway. We planned to go on sightseeing tours and explore this beautiful region that includes Nice, Cannes, and Juan-les-Pins.

The day before we left for France, I had fallen and felt some pain around my chemo port. The port is a small device that's implanted under the skin in the upper chest. It's attached to a vein to more easily deliver the chemotherapy drugs. I didn't think too much about it, but as the plane landed, the area around my port was red, tender, and hot. I said to my husband, "I think I've got an infection."

We had a tour booked that morning, so I didn't worry about it. When I woke up the next morning, I couldn't turn my neck. But my tough, I-can-push-through-anything persona won the draw, and we went on another tour.

As the tour ended, I asked the tour guide where I could go to see a doctor. She was amazing. She helped me download an app and book an appointment on the spot.

The doctor had me go for bloodwork, and after receiving the results, I ended up seeing the top doctor in the South of France for infectious diseases.

He took blood from my port, and as he put the needle in, pus poured out. He confirmed that I definitely had an infection of some sort. They immediately put me on antibiotics while waiting for the test results, but meanwhile, the redness was creeping up my neck.

The blood work came back and confirmed that it was a staph infection. We contacted my doctor in Toronto, and it was decided that my doctor would remove the port when we returned home. It turns out that the staph infection was a result of my port not being cleaned properly. The doctors in France were incredible, and even though it threw a tiny wrench in our plans, we were still able to have a wonderful time. I got the care I needed, and we finished our trip.

We returned to Toronto on Sunday, and Monday morning, I was at the hospital bright and early. The port was removed within two hours of arriving, and the doctor said the infection was gone.

The lesson here is that even though you have cancer, you don't have to stop living your life. In fact, you shouldn't. It was important to me to celebrate my last chemo treatment, but I was still cautious. I listened to my body—I knew something was wrong with my port, and my daughter, the medical student, confirmed what I felt. So I got the help I needed. We had to change our plans a little, but we went with the flow, and ended up creating fun memories.

I didn't test myself with hard things because I had a death wish; I wanted to live. But you never know what the future holds. I was doing everything I could to survive cancer, but if surviving wasn't in the cards, I wanted to live what was left of my life to the fullest. I wanted to experience everything. And our trip to France is a vacation I'll always remember.

I know not everyone will have the opportunity to travel as I did, but I encourage you to find ways to enjoy your life, even if it's going to your favorite restaurant or getting a manicure. No matter how small, capturing a few moments of happiness can sustain you amid the chaos of appointments, treatments, and days when you don't feel like getting out of bed. The key is to take advantage of those days when you have more energy. Just remember that there is a fine line between courage and carelessness. I always traveled with someone, so I was never alone, and I checked in with my body before any strenuous activity.

Make a Bucket List

If you haven't made a bucket list, grab your Healing Playbook, add a new tab, and make a list of all the things you want to do.

Your list doesn't have to be filled with outrageous, crazy things. It could be as simple as wanting to have fresh flowers in your home, trying a new food, taking a cooking class, doing the cancer mud run, renting an electric bike for a day, or going to a live show.

It doesn't matter what it is as long as it's something that brings you joy and allows you to feel like yourself again. It's important to your healing journey to give yourself space to recharge. It's what keeps your soul going when the treatments become unbearable. So take that trip, climb that mountain, and buy those flowers because you can! You deserve it.

Define Your Personal Mission Statement for This Season

Good leaders lead with vision. Even in a crisis, a company's mission statement can inform leadership on how to proceed to have the best outcome for the company, stockholders, and employees. A mission statement keeps the company aligned when hard times arrive.

The same principle applies in healing. When life feels out of control, having a personal mission statement brings everything back into focus. It reminds you that you're not just a patient, but a human with a divine purpose.

If you've never created a personal mission statement, it can feel overwhelming, but it's really just a matter of asking yourself questions.

- How do I want to show up for myself during this journey?
- What matters most to me at this moment and why?

- What inner strength or belief helps me keep going when I feel like giving up?

- What meaning or purpose do I want to create from this experience?

- What are the qualities I rely on most when I face challenges?

- Which core values guide my decisions, relationships, and healing?

- What does thriving look like for me—emotionally, spiritually, and beyond survival?

As you answer these questions, you'll begin to see what truly matters to you. Maybe success in your cancer journey means being present with your family. Maybe it's finding peace in the uncertainty of it all. Or perhaps it's taking that trip you've always dreamed of.

Write down whatever comes to your mind, and let it guide you to one clear thought about how you want to define this moment in your life. Are you striving for resilience, courage, or purpose? Do you want to focus on sharing a legacy of strength and survival? Would you like your cancer story to inspire others?

Form your ideas into a strong, powerful statement that you can return to again and again whenever life feels unbearable. You are still the CEO of your life, even in this crisis, so step up and lead with vision.

Examples of Personal Mission Statements

If you're having trouble forming your mission statement (brain fog, anyone?), I've got a few examples for you. Feel free to borrow any of these, or cobble together a statement that feels true to you.

- To greet each day with courage and grace, proving that true strength lies in facing fear and choosing to keep going.

- To live with presence and purpose, using my journey to uplift others and remind them that hope, humor, and love are more powerful than illness.

- To embody healing in every breath, nurturing my body, mind, and spirit as one whole.

- To let this experience shape me, not define me, and to move forward with intention and clarity.

- To transform survival into a legacy of courage, kindness, quiet strength, and authentic living that inspires others to fight for what matters.

- To seek joy in small moments, laughter through difficult times, and gratitude in every heartbeat.

- To live fully and fearlessly, savoring each moment as a sacred gift.

- To lead by example, showing that healing is not just surviving but also thriving with meaning and purpose.

- To be a steady light for others on this path, proving that even in chaos, I can choose how I live.

- To trust the process, honor my body's wisdom, and walk in faith, knowing my purpose is still being written.

Your Prescription for Rest

Healing looks different for everyone. Some days, you'll have more energy than you know what to do with; others will lay you out cold. Just know that it's okay to rest. Take a nap, say no to what drains you, and rest when you need to.

I talk a lot about fighting, but every good fighter knows when it's time to stand down. Healing takes place when you allow your body and mind to rest. Sometimes that means staying in bed all day. Sometimes it means taking active rest days. Either way, you don't have to push yourself to the limit to prove you're strong because I, for one, already know you're a champion.

CHAPTER 12

Live as a Healing Rebel

As patients complete their cancer treatment, they often get to ring a brass bell in the hospital to celebrate being cancer-free and to symbolize the end of treatments. Ringing the bell represents the struggle and the victory of overcoming cancer, and it can feel empowering.

My story went a little differently from most. I did not get to ring the bell because my hospital didn't have one. In March, eight days after my last chemo treatment when I should have been celebrating the end of chemotherapy, I was at my mom's funeral, delivering her eulogy.

After chemotherapy, I was put on an immunotherapy treatment called Herceptin. Once again, as I completed the Herceptin treatment in October, I didn't have the opportunity to celebrate that milestone because I had lost my father to Alzheimer's and was, for the second time that year, delivering a eulogy.

During a time when I should have been celebrating, I didn't have a moment to breathe, and I never got to step over the finish line and acknowledge that I reached the goal post. I found it to be very anticlimactic, and maybe that's why part of me feels like I'm still not done. Although I beat cancer—I won, and I have the scars to prove it—I'm still fighting to live a "normal" life.

That's the truth for many cancer patients. Even when you ring that bell, the "end" isn't really the end.

When "The End" Isn't the End

Today, my scans are clear and there is no evidence of disease (NED) in my body, but that doesn't stop me from worrying that it will come back. And it doesn't mean I'm completely healed and can resume my former life.

People often use the terms "no evidence of disease" and "remission" interchangeably, but those terms don't mean the same thing. Once your scans are clear, and you begin the "after cancer" treatments, you're in a window of NED that lasts until you finish the additional treatments and five years have passed with clear scans. It's only then that you're considered to be in full remission.

With the completion of a successful chemotherapy treatment, I've closed the chapter on fighting cancer, but now I'm in the next chapter: the "after cancer" chapter. For me, this is the hardest part. You would think that going through chemo and all of its side effects would be the hardest thing about fighting cancer, but it's not.

The "after cancer" chapter is different for everyone, but can include additional treatments such as radiation, Herceptin, Zometa, tamoxifen, or aromatase inhibitors (AI). Since I'm high risk, I'm currently on a protocol of AI, which will hopefully prevent the cancer from coming back. All of those treatments come with their own goody bag of fun side effects like chronic joint pain, chronic fatigue, and chronic brain fog.

Each of those side effects alone is hard enough to deal with, but when they all hit at once, it can completely wreck your day—or year. Each symptom intensifies the others, so that when you're tired, the pain is worse, and your memory bolts out the door. I call it the triple Venn.

As a result of chemotherapy treatments, being catapulted into early menopause, and taking AI, these symptoms became the chronic story of my life.

Symptoms caused by:
Chemotherapy, Menopause, and
Aromatase Inhibitors

chronic
pain

chronic
fatigue

chronic
brain
fog

I could also add a fourth circle to the Venn diagram: Post Traumatic Stress Disorder (PTSD). I'm dealing with PTSD from the tsunami of traumatic events that all happened within three years:

- Mik suffered a heart attack while I was flying home.
- I lost my sister to esophageal and breast cancer.
- I was diagnosed with breast cancer.
- We were victims of a home invasion.
- I lost my mom to metastatic brain cancer.
- I lost my dad to Alzheimer's.

Through it all, my brain continues to fire on all cylinders, and my nervous system remains heightened, stuck in fight or flight mode. In the back of my mind, I'm still waiting for the other shoe to drop. *Will the cancer come back?* It's hard to center yourself and calm your nervous system when you've been through hell.

The thing is, after you "beat cancer," your support group moves on. On the outside, I look like I'm better. I look healthier. I've gained back some of the weight I lost, and my hair grew back. But on the inside, I still struggle. I look "normal" and seem to function just fine. But underneath it all, I know I still have at least 10 more years of taking medications, dealing with the side effects of those medications, and staying vigilant. I still wake up every morning with the never-ending fear that cancer has returned. Maybe I outran and outsmarted it this time, but it's waiting in the shadows, looking for a chance to strike again.

It's a mind fuck—the worst kind of mental game. You're chasing the person you once were, and you know you'll never be that person again. But still, you hope. They tell you to embrace your "new normal." I hate that phrase. But acceptance is something all thrivers have to deal with. Today, I'm making myself better than I was before because I know that what's important today—life, family, friends—is more important than chasing a career and breaking that glass ceiling.

Cancer changes your life irrevocably, and part of that is the way people look at you after you've beaten cancer. The outside world expects you to celebrate, but it's hard to celebrate when you still feel like you're getting knocked around the ring. The chronic joint pain, chronic fatigue, and chronic brain fog are daily reminders that you're not the same person you were before you joined the C Club. And then, of course, there's the survivor's guilt.

Survivor's Guilt: My New Accessory

Two women who taught me how to live, laugh, fight, and navigate life with style and grace are gone. They both lost their fight with cancer. But I didn't. I survived.

So now I sit on the grass between two granite headstones, my mom's and my sister's, with a cemetery picnic of crackers and brie, and I talk to them. I tell them stories about my life and feel sad that they didn't get to finish their story. I ask them questions they'll never answer. And even though I know they can't hear me, I still hope that somehow they know I'm here, so I raise my glass and toast the good times.

That's what survivor's guilt looks like—wondering why I get to sit in the sun while they're…not here.

I'm alive. Repeat it with me: I'm alive! And that's a beautiful truth, yet it's heavier than people realize. When you survive cancer, everyone wants a Hollywood ending. A slow-motion walk down a red-carpeted hospital hallway, ringing the bell to a cacophony of applause and cheers. But beyond the party is the part no one talks about: not everyone gets to ring the bell. Some people die. That messes with your brain and makes you wonder, *why me? Why did I get to stay, and they didn't?* Which leads to more questions: Am I grateful enough? How am I making a difference with the life I was given? This quiet, persistent guilt can pressure you to make your survival mean something.

What do you do when survivor's guilt descends like a little black rain cloud?

You acknowledge it and let yourself feel the unfairness without trying to fix it. You honor those who didn't make it by not wasting the chance you got. You light candles, say their names, tell their stories, and remember that grief and gratitude can sit at the same table. You keep living not because you're fearless, but because you can. And that's reason enough.

Through it all, be gentle with yourself. Some days you'll feel like you can conquer the world; other days a song on the radio or a whiff of a scent on the air will catch you off guard and plunge you into a spiral of self-doubt. Please know that you are not alone. Sometimes the bravest thing you can do is to sit quietly, breathe, and let yourself feel the weight and the wonder of the miracle of being here.

If you're experiencing survivor's guilt, please connect with other cancer survivors in a support group or seek professional help. Your doctor or hospital can recommend a good option for you. Your survivorship program will have resources for you. Of course, I would love to see you in the Healing Rebel Community on Instagram @farlaefros.

Welcome to the Survivorship Program

After sitting in a fluorescent-lit waiting room for three uncomfortable hours, my oncologist welcomed me into her office, smiled, and said, "You've done so well. We're moving you into a different phase of care. It's time to transition into the survivorship program." She was breaking up with me. Cue the '80s breakup soundtrack.

Ah, yes. Survivorship. That mythical land where you're supposedly healed and thriving—even though every little ache or weird pain sets off alarm bells in your head: *Is it cancer?*

She said, "a different phase of care," but what I heard was that the Farla Project is now complete. File closed. I was being handed off like hand-me-down leg warmers—and after everything we'd been through together! I told her I wasn't leaving. She had to keep me as a patient.

But all joking aside, survivorship can be a very lonely road to walk because at this point, with the cancer gone, you don't look sick. You look healthy again. Maybe you've regained some weight, your hair has grown back, and you have a little more energy. On the outside, all seems fine. But on the inside, you are still filled with fear that the cancer will come back; that it's just hiding in some small corner of your body waiting for an opportunity to steal the spotlight again.

Anything out of the ordinary can be cause for concern. A headache is never a headache; it's a quickening of the pulse, a warning bell. A cold is never a cold; it's a possible sequel. And that ache in your side spurs an internet all-nighter, falling down rabbit holes when all you really needed was a good night's sleep and possibly an antacid.

Navigating Survivorship Like a Healing Rebel

Survivorship is not for the faint of heart. Remember when I said the post-cancer phase is harder in a lot of ways than the cancer-treatment phase? This is what I mean. At this point in your journey, you may not have the support from family and friends that you did during your treatment when everyone rallied around you. For them, the race is over. For you, you're still out on the course looking for the finish line.

In survivorship, you still need care, you still need answers, and you still need to advocate for yourself. That means you still need your Healing Rebel Playbook.

But now, instead of tracking chemo treatments, you're tracking symptoms from your new treatment protocols. You're still focusing on good nutrition and exercise, and keeping your doctors in the loop about how you feel.

The Executive Board you assembled in step 2 of the Healing Rebel Protocol will probably look a little different now too.

While some Board Members will play a smaller role, others will come to the forefront, and you'll lean on them more for advice.

Your cancer survivorship program becomes a member of your Executive Board by default. Your survivorship program might look different from mine, or from others you know, but generally, these programs help you manage the physical and mental side effects of your cancer journey. They help you monitor for recurrence and promote overall health through nutrition, exercise, and mental health support. They can even help support you through returning to work or navigating the insurance labyrinth.

The survivorship program is just another chapter of The C Club, but at least this club comes with more hope. For me, cancer was the hardest thing I've ever had to do, but in it, I found strength.

Cancer Is Now My Strength

If this chapter felt heavy to you, it did to me too. But as I write this, I can't quiet the voice in my head telling me: *You are a badass!*

I hope you have that voice in your head too. Because once you've been through cancer or another life-altering illness, you don't have time to feel sorry for yourself. We got a second chance and I don't know about you, but I'm going to revel in it, rejoice in it, and "party like it's 1999!"

At first, cancer felt like a thief. It crept in uninvited and made itself at home in my body. It started taking things without my permission: sleep, energy, appetite, and plans. And it didn't stop there. It took my hair, my eyelashes and eyebrows, my breasts, my fallopian tubes, and my ovaries. It stole parts of my identity so that when I looked in the mirror, I didn't even recognize myself. (I still don't like mirrors.)

But slowly, with each chemo treatment and with each scan that showed we were beating cancer into submission, I realized something: Cancer wasn't going to break me; it would rebuild me. Not into who I was before, but into someone I never knew I could be.

I used to think strength was holding it all together with a full work calendar, a toddler, and red-eye flights. Tight abs and good hair days were a bonus.

Now, I know strength looks like waking up in a body that hurts and showing up anyway. It looks like walking into a doctor's office knowing what I want to say, and not giving up when my brain won't come up with the right words. It looks like laughing when I want to cry, and sometimes crying anyway.

Strength comes from sharing my story with others who are going through the hardest fight of their lives, giving them hope with a side of humor just so they can smile again for a few minutes.

I stopped seeing cancer as a curse the day I realized it gave me permission to do things I rarely granted myself before. Things like

- resting without guilt,
- saying "no" like it's a full sentence (because it is),

- exclaiming "hell yes!" to what actually brings me joy, and
- setting boundaries without apology.

I may have survivor's guilt, but I also have survivor's grit. Cancer gave me that. Now, when I walk into a room, I'm not trying to prove anything. I already have. I am living proof of what happens when a woman refuses to go quietly—and instead shows up with scars and sass.

So, no, cancer is not my weakness. It's my strength—the spark that fuels my fire. The bonfire that says, "This rebel's just getting started."

Wanna join the party? Pull up a chair. I've got a front-row seat saved for you.

Curtain Call: Wear Your Scars Proudly

As someone who loves fashion and looking runway-ready, you might think I'd want to cover up my scars. But I don't. I wear them proudly because they are part of who I am now. I'm a survivor and although not all survivors have scars on the outside, I do. If anyone asks about them, I tell them my story.

Our scars symbolize that we've been through the wringer and are still standing, but it's okay if you're not ready to let the world see your scars yet. There are other ways to celebrate your victory.

I wear a necklace with a pendant of the breast cancer ribbon and my name on it. It reminds me that I'm not just a survivor; I'm a thriver. When I feel like I'm too tired to face the day, it's a gentle reminder of my strength.

Cancer scars, pink ribbons, and other symbols also act as a signal to others who may be going through the same thing that you're a member of The C Club too. It signifies that you've been to battle and come out on the other side.

Whenever I'm out in the world, my eye is automatically drawn to the telltale signs of another cancer survivor. Just know that I see you, and I'm proud of you. Even though living in the "after" is hard, keep fighting, keep researching, and keep advocating for yourself. If you need help, I'm here. I might be wearing my wig because sometimes I'm crazy like that, but I'm here for you.

What Cancer Taught Me

When I look back at the woman who first heard the words, "You have cancer," I almost don't recognize her. She was always on the go, carrying entire companies on her shoulders, with a Birkin bag slung over her wrist.

She could walk into any crisis, gather information, and make a plan to turn it around. She was a fixer; a strategic leader companies called when they didn't know how to fix the mess they were in.

But cancer didn't care about my résumé. It didn't care about how many fires I've put out or how many companies I've saved. *It didn't care that I wasn't done yet.*

And as much as I hated to admit it, control over everything in my life was just an illusion. Cancer forced me to see that with brutal clarity. But what this journey taught me is that strategy is not an illusion; it's real. It gives you something to hold onto when the sliding door closes on a chapter of your life. Strategy keeps you calm when control is gone.

That realization was the spark I needed. Just because cancer demanded a seat at the table didn't mean I had to let it speak. Now, more than ever, I realized that strategy, however messy, was a strength. It gave me power to move forward, but most of all, it gave me peace.

One thing I learned is that fixing is easy. Fixing keeps you in control. But it's mechanical, like checking items off a list. Feeling is the hard part. It requires trust—in yourself and in your care team. Feeling is human. It's messy and takes a lot of vulnerability, but leaning into your imperfect humanity is where true healing happens.

The Healing Rebel is who I became when I stopped pretending that I could power through cancer the same way I powered through board meetings. I realized cancer wasn't something I could do after hours or on the weekends like a part-time job. The Healing Rebel is the part of me who understood she had to let go of her past identity and step into a new one. She's the part of me who learned how to sit with discomfort, breathe through the unfamiliar, and allow growth to happen slowly and steadily.

She's the part of me that now leads with presence and gratitude.

Gratitude and Grief: Both Belong At the Table

I'm deeply grateful for science and innovation. I'm so thankful for the doctors and nurses who treated me with kindness and compassion, even as I questioned everything they told me. With the enduring support of my entire care team, including family, friends, and my Executive Board, I made it through the toughest "project" of my life. I couldn't have done it without this support system—for the people who showed up and the ones who stayed.

But I also grieve. I grieve the loss of the life I had before cancer. I grieve the loss of my breasts and nipples, my ovaries, my fallopian tubes, my eyebrows, my hair, and eyelashes—parts that no woman should have to give up. I grieve for the people who fought but didn't get to stay, and for the versions of myself I had to let go of in order to move forward. When I look in the mirror, all I see are scars. It hurts to remember who I once was.

Gratitude and grief both matter. If you feel both, it just means you're doing exactly what thrivers do: navigating the reality of being alive after fighting something that could have ended your life.

I Am Not the Same Woman, and That's Okay

I am not the same woman who strode into that first chemotherapy treatment wearing designer shoes and carrying a planner. The simplicity of the question "How are you?" contradicts the complexity of my reality. On the surface, I may appear well—I continue to exercise, eat well, and look put together. Yet, beneath the facade lies a patchwork of profound losses and daily struggles that I can't seem to put into words.

Cancer not only altered my appearance, but it also stripped away parts of my identity. Each loss is a permanent reminder of the sacrifices I made so that I could stay another day, and each new day is a testament to my resilience.

So, how am I? Honestly, some days I'm not great, but I'm making the best of it. I may never return to the person I was before cancer, but I've come to accept this new version of myself.

The person I was before, well, she did her job and got me through the sliding door. She strategized, cried, and fought like hell. She's a survivor.

But now, it's my turn to take us through the next phase: thriving in survivorship and beyond.

The same is true for you too. Do you feel changed? I hope you do. I hope you let yourself evolve into a stronger, wiser version of yourself. My goal in writing this book was to prepare you for your fight, guide you through it one decision at a time, and get you ready for what's next.

Let's take a look back at how far we've come.

The Healing Rebel Journey

Throughout the book, my goal has been simple: to give you the tools to advocate for yourself and the courage to find your voice.

It all started with the shock of diagnosis; the moment when the earth tilts. I showed you how to take command from day one, even if you felt like you were walking on shifting sand.

In part 1, we moved from panic to purpose by reclaiming our mindset. We learned to lead through fear instead of being led by it. With leadership energy, we overcame hurdles and armed ourselves with Power Moves. We realized that hope is not a strategy, and what can happen when you're not informed.

In part 2, we built our operating system for healing: The Healing Rebel Protocol. Within the six steps of the protocol, I gave you the tools and strategies designed to guide decision-making and help you advocate for yourself. You organized your care, built your team, and created your Playbook for Healing, all while grounding yourself in the three foundations from which to build your comeback: staying positive, trusting your intuition, and building mental resilience.

In part 3, we talked about ways to strengthen your body and mind so that you could rest, recharge, and live fully. Finally, we talked about what it means to live as a healing rebel: to persevere through survivor's guilt and the survivorship program, wearing your scars proudly.

The final lesson is that cancer doesn't end when treatment does. But neither does the strength, wisdom, or resilience you've built along the way. I hope you've been able to find gratitude in the process.

From diagnosis to survivorship, this book has been about one thing: taking back control, one decision at a time, and leading your comeback with confidence and courage.

Your Next Mission as a Healing Rebel

You've made it to the end of this book, but you're not at the end of your journey. Whether you just got the call that changed everything in an instant, or you're standing in the haze of chemo fog, know that you're in the right place.

Now, it's your turn to apply the Healing Rebel Protocol to whatever comes next: treatment, survivorship, managing uncertainty, or rebuilding your life piece by piece.

Start simple, but start now.

- Pause Before You Panic: No matter where you are, take a moment to ground yourself before making any decisions.

- Build your Executive Board: Find your people—the ones who stand by you, take copious notes, and remind you of who you are.

- Conduct your audit: Gather facts and figures so you know what to advocate for. Clarity gives you confidence and reduces fear.

- Ask questions: Every question you ask takes you one step closer to understanding the illness you're dealing with and the path to getting through it.

- Create your Healing Playbook: This is your command center, a personalized comeback strategy. Update it regularly, take it to every meeting, and share it with your Executive Assistant.

You Are the CEO of Your Healing

This book is for every woman who's ever whispered, "I can't do this," and then did it anyway. It's for the ones who got up when their bodies screamed, who laughed in the waiting rooms, and who made peace with the mirror and the scars.

You are that woman. You are a Healing Rebel. You don't have to wait for permission or for someone else to step in and rescue you. As you move forward into whatever comes next, remember this: You have the knowledge and power to lead the way. And I, for one, can't wait to see your comeback.

Connect with Me

Connect with me on Instagram @farlaefros and Substack @farlaefros, and join the Healing Rebel CA Community.

APPENDIX

As I wrote this book, I envisioned it becoming a reference book where you could revisit the Healing Rebel Protocol any time you needed to. I'd love nothing more than for you to highlight your favorite parts and dog-ear the pages—unless it's a library book, of course.

I also wanted to provide a few more tools and resources in a place that's easy to find, so I'm putting all the extras right here for you. These resources will help set you up for success as you command your comeback. Please keep in mind that I am not affiliated with any of these resources. I'm simply sharing the tools I've used or learned about.

SAMPLE AGENDA

Taking an agenda to your appointments is the ultimate Power Move. Here's what to include:

- Date
- Name of doctor
- Reason for appointment
- Questions
- Symptoms
- Medications
- Allergies
- Test results

Sample Calendar of Appointments

A calendar is helpful to see your appointments at a glance. You can use a calendar or keep it in list form:

- Date
- Type of appointment
- Time
- Location
- Doctor
- Driver

Sample Side Effects Tracking Sheet

It's important to keep track of side effects so you can address them at your next meeting. A spreadsheet works great for this, or you can use a notebook. Either way, you'll want to include:

- Date
- Treatment
- Side effects
- Activity or workouts

Sample Family Genetics Sheet

Having your family's medical history in one place makes it easier for you and your doctors to identify where your risks lie. A simple family genetics spreadsheet could include:

- Name
- Relationship
- Disease type
- Age at diagnosis
- Treatment
- Date of death
- Cause of death

RESOURCES

This is a short list of some of the resources I've come across. Some I've used, some I haven't. Your doctor and hospital can help you find resources in your area, including cancer support groups and classes.

The following community platforms can help with sharing information, posting updates, and asking for help:

- CaringBridge
- Lotsa Helping Hands
- Caring Village

To help with communication, try one of these texting apps:

- GroupMe
- Signal
- WhatsApp

A food scanner app can help you avoid unwanted ingredients. Try one of the following:

- Yuka
- Bobby Approved
- Olive Holistic Food Scanner

The following mindfulness apps can help manage stress:

- Insight Timer
- Smiling Mind
- Headspace
- Calm

A Life and Legacy Planner can be an amazing resource. My Banyan Life is a digital planner that works well, and you don't have to be tech-savvy to use it. Paper planners are also available. Just search the internet for "end-of-life planner."

Cancer Information and Treatment Resources

- TYRER-Cuzick Risk Assessment Calculator, also known as the IBIS (International Breast Cancer Intervention Study) risk assessment, uses your personal family history to estimate your risk of developing breast cancer.
  - » Everyone must do a lifetime risk assessment. The results will tell you if you are at high risk and need to speed up testing. If your results are over 20%, then you need to pay attention and get more testing done, including genetic testing.
- The Yerbba Report can help you understand your breast cancer treatment options.
- CTOAM (Cancer Treatment Options and Management Inc) is a cancer care research and advocacy specialist company that helps cancer patients by using the most current medical science.

Additionally, the following cancer research groups are helpful:

- American Cancer Society
- Canadian Cancer Society
- Cancer Research UK

Newsletters, Podcasts, and YouTube

Farla Efros Substack

Read more about my story, how I'm dealing with "after cancer," and what's next for me on my Substack at https://Substack.com/@farlaefros.

Dr. Erica Ainsworth, Breast Cancer Thriver & Chiropractor

- @breast-cancer-rehab
- Thriver Q&A with Farla

Yerbba Breast Cancer

- @yerbba

SHE MD Podcast

- SheMDpodcast.com

Social Media: Facebook Groups and Instagram

Facebook Groups are a great place to learn information that your doctor or pharmacist may not tell you. Go to Facebook Groups and search for your type of cancer.

For instance, one time my pharmacist switched the brand of one of my medications without telling me. I had horrible side effects and didn't know why. In the Facebook group, another woman talked about brand switching and how you may react differently to the same medication from a different brand.

I went to my pharmacist, and he confirmed that the brand had been switched. I checked the timing, and it corresponded to when my symptoms changed. This is why it's so important to know what medication you're taking and to always keep track of your symptoms.

You can learn so much from Facebook groups, and the community is great, but take care to protect your mental health. If you find that a group feels negative or depressing, don't spend too much time there.

On Instagram, search for and follow accounts that post about your type of cancer or cancer survivor stories. For breast cancer, you could follow:

- Breast Cancer Now
- BreastCancer.Org
- @susangkomen
- @cancer.survivor.stories

ACKNOWLEDGEMENTS

Healing is never a solo act, no matter how fiercely independent we try to be.

To my **incredible friends**—thank you for showing up with coffee, food, dark humor, messy hugs, and unwavering love. You kept me laughing when I forgot how, and reminded me that connection heals in ways medicine never can.

To the **incredible team at Sunnybrook Hospital**—from the doctors and nurses to the technicians and support staff—thank you for your skill, compassion, and humanity. You didn't just treat my body; you cared for my spirit. You gave me hope when I had none left to borrow. A special mention to Dr. Eisen, Dr. Jerzak, Dr. Snell, Dr. Lenkov, and my PA, E. Matheson.

To **Andy**, my trainer—thank you for teaching me that movement is medicine and that strength isn't about perfection; it's about persistence. You helped me rediscover what my body can still do, even when it hurts.

To **Erica**, my chiropractor and fellow thriver—thank you for quite literally putting me back together. You understand what it means to rebuild from the inside out, and your empathy has been part of my healing.

To **every survivor,** caregiver, and soul navigating life after cancer—this book is for you. It's your permission slip to rest, to rage, to rebuild, and to rise on your own terms.

And finally, to the universe—for breaking me open just enough to let the light flood in.

Rebellion is healing. And healing, my friends, is the most rebellious act of all.

ABOUT THE AUTHOR

Farla Efros is a seasoned retail executive, cancer survivor, mother, and unapologetic truth-teller who lives in Toronto with her husband and daughter. Farla has held senior leadership roles across the retail industry, including President of HRC Retail Advisory (part of Accenture Retail Strategy), Interim CEO of True Religion Brand Jeans, and Executive Vice President & Chief Merchandising Officer at Office Depot. Known for her sharp insights into consumer trends, she has been a frequent guest on BNN Bloomberg, offering expert analysis on retail strategy and the evolving marketplace.

After a high-powered career in business and retail, her life took a dramatic turn when she was diagnosed with aggressive breast cancer in 2023—a year that also brought unimaginable personal loss.

What followed was a journey through surgeries, chemotherapy, hormone therapy, and soul-rattling grief…but also radical resilience, dark humor, and a fierce refusal to disappear.

Through her platform The Healing Rebel CA, Farla shares the raw, real, and often hilarious side of life during and after cancer—not just survival, but the messy, painful, and surprisingly beautiful path of learning to live fully again. Her writing blends sharp wit with emotional honesty, calling out the clichés and celebrating imperfect healing with defiance and heart. Farla shares her story and strategy for reclaiming agency, building community, and living with courage and authenticity.

Farla writes to connect, to comfort, and to remind every survivor: You're not alone—and you don't have to be graceful about it.

9 781967 587872